The Manager's Survival Guide

Other titles in the Briefcase Books series include:

Customer Relationship Management by Kristin Anderson and Carol Kerr

Communicating Effectively by Lani Arredondo

Performance Management by Robert Bacal

Recognizing and Rewarding Employees by R. Brayton Bowen

Motivating Employees by Anne Bruce and James S. Pepitone

Six Sigma for Managers by Greg Brue

Leadership Skills for Managers by Marlene Caroselli

Negotiating Skills for Managers by Steven P. Cohen

Effective Coaching by Marshall J. Cook

Conflict Resolution by Daniel Dana

Project Management by Gary R. Heerkens

Managing Teams by Lawrence Holpp

Hiring Great People by Kevin C. Klinvex, Matthew S. O'Connell, and Christopher P. Klinvex

Retaining Top Employees by J. Leslie McKeown

Empowering Employees by Kenneth L. Murrell and Mimi Meredith

Presentation Skills for Managers by Jennifer Rotondo and Mike Rotondo

The Manager's Guide to Business Writing by Suzanne D. Sparks

Skills for New Managers by Morey Stettner

Interviewing Techniques for Managers by Carolyn P. Thompson

Managing Multiple Projects by Michael Tobis and Irene P. Tobis

To learn more about titles in the Briefcase Books series go to
www.briefcasebooks.com
You'll find the tables of contents, downloadable sample chapters, information on the authors, discussion guides for using these books in training programs, and more.

A
Briefcase
Book

The Manager's Survival Guide

Morey Stettner

McGraw-Hill

New York Chicago San Francisco Lisbon London
Madrid Mexico City Milan New Delhi San Juan
Seoul Singapore Sydney Toronto

McGraw-Hill

A Division of The **McGraw·Hill** *Companies*

Copyright © 2002 by The McGraw-Hill Companies, Inc. All rights reserved. Printed in the United States of America. Except as permitted under the United States Copyright Act of 1976, no part of this publication may be reproduced or distributed in any form or by any means, or stored in a database or retrieval system, without the prior written permission of the publisher.

1 2 3 4 5 6 7 8 9 0 AGM/AGM 0 9 8 7 6 5 4 3 2

ISBN 0-07-139132-0

Library of Congress Cataloging-in-Publication Data applied for.

This is a CWL Publishing Enterprises Book, developed and produced for McGraw-Hill by CWL Publishing Enterprises, Inc., John A. Woods, President. For more information, contact CWL Publishing Enterprises, 3010 Irvington Way, Madison, WI 53713-3414, www.cwlpub.com. For McGraw-Hill, the sponsoring editor is Catherine Dassopoulos, and the publisher is Jeffrey Krames.

McGraw-Hill books are available at special quantity discounts to use as premiums and sales promotions, or for use in corporate training programs. For more information, please write to the Director of Special Sales, McGraw-Hill, 2 Penn Plaza, New York, NY 10128. Or contact your local bookstore.

 This book is printed on recycled, acid-free paper containing a minimum of 50% recycled de-inked fiber.

Contents

Preface   ix

1. Heeding Warning Signs   1
Planning for Worst Case   2
Battling the Three D's   3
Setting Fair Expectations   5
The Fake Problem/Real Problem Divide   7
Three Clues That Trouble's Brewing   8
When the Ethical Line Blurs   11
Manager's Checklist for Chapter 1   13

2. Profile of a Problem: The Six Stages   15
Stage 1: The Kindling Fire   16
Stage 2: The Close Brush with Doom   18
Stage 3: Multiple Outbreaks   21
Stage 4: Blaming, Denying, and Sniping   22
Stage 5: Acknowledging the Scope   24
Stage 6: Mobilizing Action   26
Manager's Checklist for Chapter 2   27

3. Jumping from Problem to Solution   28
Four Steps to the Promised Land   29
Acting vs. Stewing   34
Seeking Wise Counsel   36
Generating Group Buy-In   38
Manager's Checklist for Chapter 3   40

4. Preventing Misunderstandings   41
Listening to Learn   42
Where's Your Receipt?   44
Culprits of the Mind   45

"Testing 1-2-3, ... Testing"   47
Learn How to "Groda"   48
Rushing into Trouble   50
Avoiding Body Language Traps   52
Manager's Checklist for Chapter 4   53

5. Calibrating Your Response   55
Flipping the Emotional Light Switch   56
Taking Stock: The Need for Perspective   58
Getting Past Grudges   59
The Power of Negative Thinking   61
Following de Gaulle's Rules   63
Discipline That Sinks In   66
Manager's Checklist for Chapter 5   67

6. Solving the Seven Biggest On-the-Job Conflicts   68
1. "There's Not Enough Time!"   69
2. "This Is Spiraling out of Control!"   70
3. "I Don't Trust You!"   72
4. "You Broke Your Promise!"   74
5. "I'll Win This Battle!"   75
6. "How Dare You Say That?!"   77
7. "I Know Better than You!"   78
Manager's Checklist for Chapter 6   80

7. Thinking Like a Scientist   81
Accepting the Problem   83
Writing a Problem Summary   84
Labeling the Cause   86
No BMWs Allowed Here   89
Analyze This—Then Judge It   91
Manager's Checklist for Chapter 7   93

8. Problem-Solvers vs. Problem-Creators   94
Four Problem-Creation Traps   95
Managing Your Mouth   98
Difficult? Or Just Different?   100
Learning Your Lesson   101
Seeing the Future   103
Good News, Bad News   105
Manager's Checklist for Chapter 8   106

9. **Combating the Threat of Change**   **108**
    Three Myths of Managing Change   109
    Looking Ahead in Increments   111
    When Projections Go Awry   114
    Celebrating Small Wins   115
    Surviving Upheaval at the Top   117
    Transforming Resistance to Acceptance   118
    Manager's Checklist for Chapter 9   121

10. **Motivating Employees Against All Odds**   **122**
    Stepping Back from the Fray   123
    Winning Over Lower-Level Workers   125
    Cheering from a Distance   127
    Salvaging Post-Layoff Morale   129
    Battling a More Powerful Rival   132
    Giving Feedback That Pays Off   133
    Manager's Checklist for Chapter 10   135

11. **Mapping a Problem-Prevention Plan**   **136**
    Selecting "Solution Czars"   138
    Charles Schwab's Secret   139
    Talking a Good Game   140
    Planning to Fail   142
    Skirting Three Traps   144
    Sprinting to the Finish Line   146
    Manager's Checklist for Chapter 11   148

    Index   **149**

Preface

Thousands of managers dream of becoming CEOs. But only a handful will make it.

What separates the career climbers from the others?

For starters, CEOs need people skills, political savvy, and lots of good luck. Yet there's one easy-to-overlook prerequisite that every chief executive must possess: *the ability to solve problems*—in other words, the ability to *survive* the daily onslaught of technical and people problems that require skillful analysis, intelligent decisions, and effective execution.

Surviving—and prospering—in organizations requires a keen awareness of what's wrong now (as well as what's right), what can go wrong later, and what must happen to fix it. Mediocre managers dread problems. They turn away from them, sugar-coat reality, and then wait in blissful ignorance for the other shoe to drop.

Fast-track leaders, by contrast, detect trouble early. They solicit advice, list their options, and take decisive action to extinguish potential fires before they rage uncontrollably. Their confidence and experience teach them to view problems as positives. When discussing setbacks or disappointments, most CEOs will reframe negatives. They'll say, "This presents an opportunity" or "We look forward to this challenge."

Adopting a can-do, let's-solve-this attitude pays off on many levels. It empowers your peers and employees to maintain hope and optimism in the face of mounting threats. It motivates you to muster the enthusiasm and inner strength to persevere when disasters hit. And it helps you think like a tactician, so that you take responsibility for identifying and weighing the best solutions.

Reputations are built at the bottom, not the top. As you climb the ladder, your determination to confront problems head on and attain your goals despite adversity will give you an edge in surviving organizational shake-outs and earning high-profile assignments and promotions.

Managers blossom into leaders when their bosses turn into raving fans. If you want higher-ups to champion your cause, get them to give you the ultimate compliment: *There's someone who doesn't let problems stand in the way.*

Why Read This Book?

Face it: you're going to fight off all kinds of problems as a manager. Some mishaps will result from your poor judgment, from faulty information, or from innocent mistakes. Others will just drop into your lap. You may inherit someone else's screw-up or simply wind up in the wrong place at the wrong time.

This book gives you the tools to identify problems, diagnose them, and plan the best course of action to address them. Whatever the causes of conflict—difficult employees, unreliable suppliers, spineless peers, or irate customers—the key is developing a strategy to stay calm, think clearly, and devise solutions.

Speed matters. Tackle problems quickly and you can reduce or eliminate disruptive aftershocks. You can also prevent the same frustrations from recurring in the future.

The more you prepare to solve problems, the stronger your resilience when they collapse upon you. In the pages that follow, you'll gain the knowledge and best practices to take setbacks in stride and reach for a toolbox of strategies that will ensure your survival—and success—as a manager destined for greatness.

Overview of the Book

In the first chapter, you'll learn to see into the distance to anticipate and disarm problems before they gather steam. By recognizing warning signs, rather than falling into the trap of the three

D's (downplaying, distorting, dismissing), you can set reasonable expectations for solving conflicts. You'll also develop a more watchful eye for abrupt changes in the way workers communicate, sudden disruptions of previously predictable patterns, and the hasty imposition of new, restrictive workplace rules.

Chapter 2 traces the evolution of a typical workplace problem in six stages, from the kindling fire to multiple outbreaks to the final push for action. By treating a problem as a multi-step event and separating what you can and cannot control, you gain the knowledge and confidence you need to take charge and make the right moves.

By Chapter 3, you're ready to plunge into solutions. By taking even the most formidable problems and breaking them into bite-size chunks, you can make headway against all odds. Even if you're ultimately responsible for fixing what's broken, you need allies such as a trusted advisor and your employees to give you their best advice and efforts.

Chapter 4 exposes one of the main culprits at the core of many problems—misunderstandings. That's why most leaders listen so well; they know that if they hear only what they want to hear, they may draw the wrong conclusions.

In Chapter 5, your response to problems takes center stage. You can devise speedy, brilliant, creative solutions. But if you panic, yell, or hold grudges, you sabotage yourself and divert attention from your great results.

Warning: Chapter 6 is fraught with conflict. But you're going to practice strategies to restore peace when tempers flare and referee when bickering employees threaten to come to blows. You'll learn to speak a positive language, free of war metaphors, to calm frayed nerves and lure everyone toward a mutually agreeable outcome.

Chapter 7 highlights the need to balance emotions with reason when solving problems. Using scientists as a model, you'll develop tools to gather information and evaluate it dispassionately.

There are two kinds of people—problem-solvers and problem-creators—and in Chapter 8 you'll learn about the differences. Adopt a healthy, solution-oriented mindset and you're way ahead of the game. If you react to mishaps by thinking of what's possible rather than lamenting, "Why me?," you're on the right track.

So many problems in today's workplaces are caused at least in part by organizational change. Chapter 9 confronts this threat head on. You'll gain techniques to cope with change from above and to communicate it to your employees.

Many challenges arise when managers are working with employees who are unmotivated and apathetic. Chapter 10 offers motivational tips for a range of tricky or delicate situations, from dealing with survivors of layoffs to leading your off-site, telecommuting workers to give 100%.

Finally, in Chapter 11, the discussion shifts from solving problems to preventing them. Take proactive steps to ward off mishaps and you'll save yourself countless hours of stress.

Special Features

The idea behind the books in the Briefcase Series is to give you practical information written in a friendly person-to-person style. The chapters are short, deal with tactical issues, and include lots of examples. They also feature numerous boxes designed to give you different types of specific information. Here's a description of the boxes you'll find in this book.

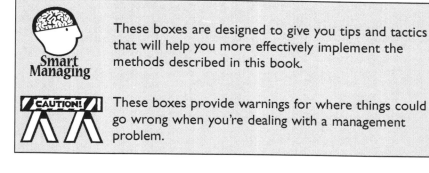

Smart Managing
These boxes are designed to give you tips and tactics that will help you more effectively implement the methods described in this book.

CAUTION!
These boxes provide warnings for where things could go wrong when you're dealing with a management problem.

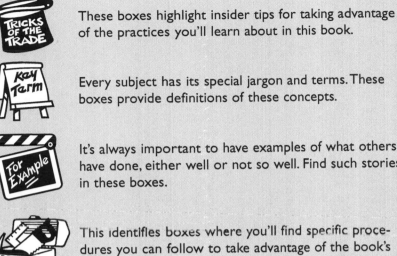

These boxes highlight insider tips for taking advantage of the practices you'll learn about in this book.

Every subject has its special jargon and terms. These boxes provide definitions of these concepts.

It's always important to have examples of what others have done, either well or not so well. Find such stories in these boxes.

This identifies boxes where you'll find specific procedures you can follow to take advantage of the book's advice.

How can you make sure you won't make a mistake when dealing with a problem? You can't, but these boxes will give you practical advice on how to minimize the possibility.

The Manager's Survival Guide

Heeding
Warning Signs

Jet fighters often fly in fours. Within these clusters, one pilot serves as the leader by flying the "No. 1" position. This individual sets the pace and largely influences whether a mission will succeed. Pilots of the second, third, and fourth jets are trained to "fly the leader's wing," meaning they must follow closely the No. 1 jet's maneuvers.

On rare occasions, all four planes will crash. Say the leader flies into a fog bank and rams the side of a mountain. Odds are the other three will do the same.

As James A. Autry writes in *Life and Work* (New York: William Morrow & Co., 1994), leaders must adopt a "think for No. 4" mindset: before they make any move, they must weigh how it'll affect the other jets behind them.

The same goes with managers. When facing problems, they must consider how their response will influence not only themselves, but everyone around them.

When you face roadblocks at work, a spotlight shines on you, whether you like it or not. Your boss wants to see if you can pass this test of your mettle. Your employees might look to you for guidance. Your colleagues wait and watch how you handle it.

Like the leader of a jet formation, your actions will have a ripple effect. By charting the right course and making smart decisions, you ensure your survival and reassure bystanders that you can withstand whatever obstacles threaten your flight path.

Planning for Worst Case

When you're driving along a highway, you might notice roadside markers proclaiming, "Points of Interest Ahead" or "Historical Site Ahead." These signs are usually positioned about a quarter of a mile before the attraction so that you can slow and stop in time.

If you're driving too fast, these signs can zip by you in a blur. That's no big loss if you didn't care about the historical sites you missed. But if you skip a yellow "Warning" or "Speed Bump" sign and continue racing obliviously down the road, you can wind up losing control of your vehicle and getting into an accident.

Problems at work crop up the same way. There are almost always signs of what's to come. But the question is whether you're observant enough to recognize those signs and take appropriate action while there's still time.

Clues of impending trouble often appear in the behavior of those around you and the topics they bring up. If a normally sunny employee begins to look forlorn and sickly, an attentive manager will inquire and offer to help. If your most prized customer's purchases start to tail off or you find yourself having to send second or third billing notices to a client who previously paid within 30 days, that may signal a dissatisfied or ailing account.

If you're the kind of driver or bus rider who habitually misses your exit, you may also find yourself ignoring early trouble signs. Daydreaming or maintaining tunnel vision can prevent you from noticing trouble afoot.

Many managers detect incipient problems and respond with

> ### Set the Dial
> If you miss trouble signs at their earliest point, they can soon balloon into huge hassles. Here's an exercise to get a head start on solving problems. As soon as you notice something's awry, think of three possible explanations:
> 1. The most innocent, harmless possibility
> 2. A relatively mild problem that's somewhat easy to manage
> 3. The worst-case scenario
> By identifying the best and worst cases and what falls in between, you create a Richter scale that registers everything from the most minor tremor to the dreaded Big One. This helps you wrap your mind around the potential severity of the problem and forces you to consider the full range of outcomes.

a wait-and-see attitude. That's understandable, but it's risky. A situation that seems seemingly insignificant can, if left untended, fester and intensify. For instance, a vendor who jokes that your organization's bureaucracy "drives me crazy" may not find the matter so funny a few weeks later when more serious foul-ups occur.

By taking trouble signs seriously, you can attempt to bring about a speedy resolution while planning for the worst. That way no matter what happens next, you're covered.

Battling the Three D's

You're on a roll. You're making headway on an important project, you've motivated your team to deliver exceptional results, and you're finalizing negotiations with a key vendor on a service contract. Everything's clicking.

That's precisely when you want to confront conflicts head on and nip them in the bud.

In my management seminars, experienced managers often warn of the dangers of overconfidence. They'll cite instances when they're in the midst of intense work and they "don't want to lose the momentum," so they shove aside evidence of problems and charge ahead. The result: minor obstacles escalate into major crises.

The time to address problems is when they first arise. That may mean doing something as simple as clarifying a rule with an employee, apologizing for an error, or resending an errant e-mail. Otherwise, you're vulnerable to the three D's of problem mismanagement: downplaying, distorting, or dismissing signs of trouble.

Downplaying. It's tempting to downplay evidence of a problem when you're focusing on other matters. But once you start downplaying signs of trouble, you can rationalize almost any mishap as a "cost of doing business" or a "blip on the radar screen."

Say you're concentrating on internal staffing issues. You're aware of a key supplier's lateness and shoddy product, but it's not at the top of your list of concerns right now so you downplay it by thinking, "It's no big deal. They'll improve." Yet when a supplier's service starts to crumble, it's likely that it will continue on a slippery slope and worsen. Speaking up now and expressing your displeasure can forestall a further erosion of service.

Distorting. Recognizing a conflict for what it is sounds easy. But some managers distort reality and perceive a problem as they see fit. They might exaggerate the importance of good news and view bad news as "a blessing in disguise." While it's often wise to maintain a positive attitude, you can go overboard if you twist genuinely troubling indicators into "good omens."

A marketing manager confessed to me how she distorted the facts about a misguided and ultimately abortive new-product rollout at her company. She orchestrated an ambitious advertising and direct mail campaign. But the early response fell far below her projections. Rather than make adjustments, she admits that she "kept wanting to believe we were on the right track" so she attributed the poor response to "a post-Sept. 11 malaise." Yet her industry's sales were soaring and her competitors were launching wildly successful new products even as hers was fizzling. Her distortion made the disappointment more palatable at the time, but it kept her from grasping the true source of the problem and learning from it.

Dismissing. If you wave away evidence of a problem, you don't have to confront it. Denial can help you cope in the short term. But it spreads. Your fellow managers and employees might follow your lead and dismiss brewing crises right under their noses. Soon you can have an entire organization that shrugs off alarming trends or refuses to listen when outsiders warn or complain of irregularities.

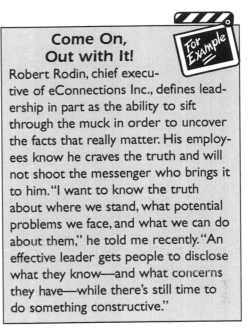

Come On, Out with It!

Robert Rodin, chief executive of eConnections Inc., defines leadership in part as the ability to sift through the muck in order to uncover the facts that really matter. His employees know he craves the truth and will not shoot the messenger who brings it to him. "I want to know the truth about where we stand, what potential problems we face, and what we can do about them," he told me recently. "An effective leader gets people to disclose what they know—and what concerns they have—while there's still time to do something constructive."

Setting Fair Expectations

When you acknowledge an obstacle in your path and take stock of it with levelheaded clarity, you're already well on your way to conquering it. The next step is setting realistic expectations so that you assign the appropriate significance to the problem.

Here's where your attitude kicks in.

If you're gloomy or fretful by nature, you might expect a problem to intensify or explode in your face any minute now and you probably won't bother to hide your fear. Others will notice you cursing, shaking your head in dismay, or sighing repeatedly. As the minutes turn to hours, you might wince in pain, lament your lot in life, and accost colleagues with "Why me?" bellyaching.

At the other extreme, unrelenting optimists often expect too much. When faced with a barrier that impedes their progress, they may look ahead with false hope that the problem will not only go away, but will never return *and* that tackling it will make them—and everyone around them—stronger as a result. That's a tall order.

If you're more centered and practical, you'll pounce on problems with unflappable ease. You'll collect data, evaluate your options, and choose the best one. You'll leave work expecting to put the problem to bed without fanfare. You know there's nothing to gain by torturing or chastising yourself.

In setting reasonable expectations for problem solving, try comparing the current challenge with ones you've faced in the past. Recall three examples of problems you encountered. Consider how you characterized them at first, what outcomes you expected, and what happened.

Were you on target? Or did your expectations prove off base? What surprised you?

Through this exercise, you can use your experience as a guide when new problems arise. Setting fair expectations keeps you on an even keel emotionally and enables you to process new information in a receptive frame of mind.

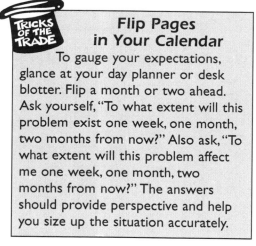

Flip Pages
in Your Calendar

To gauge your expectations, glance at your day planner or desk blotter. Flip a month or two ahead. Ask yourself, "To what extent will this problem exist one week, one month, two months from now?" Also ask, "To what extent will this problem affect me one week, one month, two months from now?" The answers should provide perspective and help you size up the situation accurately.

Setting realistic expectations largely depends on your understanding of probability. In the early stages of a problem, it helps if you can weigh a full range of outcomes— from highly likely to highly unlikely. That requires a dispassionate analysis of what variables are at play.

If you sense that a new employee has an aversion to using high-tech tools that are critical to his job, you might say to yourself, "I expect that with proper training and encouragement, he'll do fine." But his peers have lost faith in his abilities and he shows no interest in learning how these gizmos work. He also insists that he doesn't need them.

These factors should deflate your expectations, because

they make it less likely he'll respond well to training and support. Rather than blithely expect that he'll do fine, you'd manage this situation more effectively if you said, "It's *highly likely* he'll continue avoiding these high-tech tools as long as he can. It's *possible* that he'll be more willing to use them as he gets more comfortable working here and gets properly trained. It's *highly unlikely* that no matter what we do, he'll never use them the way they're supposed to be used."

The Fake Problem/Real Problem Divide

The sooner you notice signs of problems developing, the sooner you can assess what exactly you're up against. The trick is distinguishing between illusory problems—that either don't really exist or evaporate quickly on their own—and actual ones that merit your attention.

What may appear to you as a seemingly intractable mess can prove a nonevent. This can happen when you impute false motives to others, feel undue embarrassment, or blow trivial inconveniences out of proportion.

The most common cause of "pretend problems" is reading too much into others' behavior. Say Peter, a peer who corrects your grammar a few times, annoys you at first, then starts really getting on your nerves. Soon you think, "Peter wants to knock me down a peg or two. I better fight back." So you subtly undermine Peter's efforts and lambaste him when you're chatting with influential higher-ups. You don't know that Peter has been tutoring his daughter on grammar so he's especially attuned to proper and improper usage. He means no harm.

Don't jump to conclusions about why others act the way they do. Pause and withhold judgment. Give them a chance to redeem themselves. Diplomatically point out what they're doing and see how they respond. If you playfully say to Peter, "You're quite the grammar maven these days, aren't you?" he'll probably tell you it's all because he's helping his daughter with her homework. Then you'll know he's not trying to make you look stupid! That solves that.

Key Term **Projection** Grafting onto others your own anxieties or insecurities, often leading you to see these individuals in a less flattering light. For example, you may project your doubt over your ability to understand complex technical processes by presuming that technically proficient coworkers don't know what they're talking about. As a result, you disregard their advice and complain that you work among know-nothing blowhards. Projection leads you to manufacture a problem that doesn't exist.

If you're embarrassed, you might also inflame a situation to the point where you create a problem for yourself. Consider what can happen if you're delivering a presentation to your board of directors and you lose your place, show a slide upside down, or mispronounce the name of a visiting dignitary in the audience. As soon as you realize your mistake, your mind races. You think, "Now they really see me as an impostor" or "Now I've turned them against me."

In truth, however, most audiences are forgiving. Rebound from a minor blunder with aplomb and you can impress bigwigs. The only problem is in your head. Mentally berate yourself and you'll slip into a downward spiral.

Another type of fake problem occurs if you transform a minor inconvenience into a major crisis. Short-tempered or impatient managers who curse when put on hold not only induce needless stress, but they risk carrying their anger into the conversation. That in turn can trigger an entirely preventable conflict. A pseudo-problem can thus mutate into a real one if you lose your cool.

Three Clues That Trouble's Brewing

Problems rarely pop up overnight. A gradual accumulation of signs usually precedes the full-blown outbreak of a crisis. Those indicators can range from almost imperceptible changes in how others behave to more obvious red flags, such as lost sales or high employee turnover. The clues of impending problems can vary, but they normally fall into three categories:

- Changes in communication
- Pattern disruption
- New rules

Changes in Communication

Spend enough time around your peers, bosses, and employees and you'll grow accustomed to the way they speak and listen. You may fall into comfortable habits of finishing each other's sentences, reading nonverbal cues, and using certain acronyms as shorthand.

If you notice the tone or rhythm of your conversations starts to change for the worse, that can signify a problem lurking under the surface. Examples:

- An employee who used to express admiration for upper management at your firm now seems strangely reticent and hesitant to compliment anyone.
- A boss who used to look you in the eyes when giving updates on the company's financial health now fidgets and looks away when you ask, "How are our numbers doing?"
- A customer who used to exchange pleasantries with you before getting down to business now exhibits an uncharacteristically curt demeanor and rushes to get off the phone.

Such changes in communication style do not in themselves spell trouble ahead. But when you detect a loss of camaraderie or openness from someone who previously radiated warmth and good cheer, it's quite possibly an indication that something's amiss. It may have nothing to do with you and may in no way affect your job. Nevertheless, by making a mental note of when and where a person starts communicating differently, you can gain information that might expose fault lines worth examining.

Pattern Disruption

You may bemoan the predictable routines of your daily work life, but the status quo brings with it a certain steadiness and

Keep a Log

TOOLS When you first notice a distinct change in a coworker's communication style, write the day, time, and a sentence or two about the circumstances in a private journal. Keep recording your observations as further incidents arise. You may find that a typically social, high-energy, jocular employee speaks in a more reserved, withdrawn tone in the hour after the weekly management meeting—a possible sign that something's happening in those meetings to demoralize this person.

familiarity. The boring office rituals—like spending a few minutes on Monday morning with colleagues listening to them dissect the performance of their favorite professional sports teams—offer reassurance that everything's chugging along just fine.

When patterns get disrupted, it may mean trouble. Maybe a normally responsive supplier starts returning your calls a few days later rather than a few hours later or a once-reliable contract worker turns in assignments after the deadline.

A manager in one of my seminars described how he used to devote the first hour of the day (7:00 to 8:00 a.m.) to "heavy concentration work." That worked well for a while until he started getting interrupted by jittery employees coming in early to discuss job-security issues.

"That's when I sensed we might have a morale problem," he said. "Sure enough, after a few months of having my mornings shot to hell, I found out our company was going to be acquired and that would lead to layoffs."

New Rules

When restrictive rules get imposed unilaterally in your organization, it could mean something's wrong and needs fixing. And there's no guarantee a new rule will solve it.

Whether your CEO announces new quality-control compliance measures or a regulatory agency requires your company to adopt more rigid financial reporting, look beyond the immediate action to the underlying situation. What do the new rules attempt to address? What problem could result otherwise? And will the rules really prevent this problem?

The need for new rules may underscore a more serious failing in your organization. Read between the lines to determine what's at stake.

When the Ethical Line Blurs

The most respected managers skip the ambiguities and rationalizations when it comes to principled behavior. They set a high bar for their ethics—and this commitment positively influences those around them. They know that ethical compromises lead to more compromises, so they operate well within the boundaries of what's right.

If you start seeing signs of unethical or ethically questionable behavior among your bosses and colleagues, it almost guarantees real problems ahead. Watch for the following omens.

Jumbled priorities. When the interests of your employees, customers, and the general public take a back seat to the narrow interests of individuals within your company, that's a combustible mix. Example: other managers start bragging to you about how they pad their expense reports—and encourage you to do the same.

Misguided incentives. Executives who reward dubious behavior will soon find themselves managing in an ethical sinkhole. Dangling bonuses or other perks for employees who cut corners to meet production goals may produce short-term gains at a steep long-term cost. Example: sales managers at some life insurance companies pressure their agents to convert customers from one cash-value policy to another. When this practice began to spread in the early 1990s, only a handful of managers spoke out. Within a few years, however, some of the nation's largest insurers were admitting massive fraud and negotiating huge settlements with state regulators.

Abuse of power. If the head of your division takes kickbacks from vendors, you may shrug and figure that's "just the way it is." And in many industries, there's a high tolerance for what managers rationalize as "customary" payments. But what

Test 1: Ethical Quiz

Setting a high ethical standard in the office seems simple, but gray areas abound. Answer these questions to identify potential trouble spots:

Yes No   Have I discovered my peers or bosses doing something that's ethically questionable?

Yes No   Over the last year, have my peers or bosses instructed me not to tell anyone about something that they did?

Yes No   Am I doing anything to others that I wouldn't want them to do to me?

Yes No   If my beloved grandparents could watch me at work for a week, would they object to any ethical lapses of mine? Would they object to the ethical behavior of others?

Yes No   If a reporter followed me around with a video camera all week, would I be ashamed of anything in the footage? Would others be ashamed?

Yes No   Do I have a queasy feeling that there's something ethically questionable going on behind my back?

Yes No   If I led youngsters on a tour of my workplace, would they see anything that I wouldn't be proud for them to see?

seems harmless and justifiable today can blossom into a front-page news story tomorrow.

It's easier to rid yourself of ethical dilemmas by anticipating the kind of issues you and your colleagues will face—and taking a proactive approach to address them. If your organization has a comprehensive, written code of conduct, an ethics officer (or ombudsman), or a formal ethics training program in place, you're ahead of the game. But most companies, especially small and mid-size businesses, do not codify their ethical practices formally.

If your organization lacks ethical training or published guidelines, think of potential conflicts of interest and initiate dialogues with your colleagues on how to deal with them. Consider these four hot spots.

Protecting proprietary information. No one associated with your organization (including suppliers, customers, and consultants) should disclose proprietary information without proper authorization. All such materials and documents should be protected and secure.

Gifts, meals, entertainment. Employees should not accept freebies of any kind if it adversely affects their decision-making or taints their ability to be objective.

Company assets. Employees should safeguard their employer's assets—funds, property, information, databases, customer lists, records, etc. As a rule, employees should not profit from these assets for personal benefit unless such assets have been approved for general, public use.

Outside activities. As flexible work arrangements gain popularity, many full-time employees moonlight in other businesses. This can raise a problem if any of them spend less time and pay less attention to their primary jobs. You may want to require employees to get your written consent to engage in outside jobs or activities that pose a possible conflict of interest or divert resources from their full-time employment.

Listen for Warning Bells

Trouble's on the horizon if you hear anyone at work use such phrases as these:

- "Oh, no one will ever know...."
- "Stop! I don't want to know any more. Just get it done."
- "It's fine. Everyone does it."
- "It's easy to hide."
- "No one's getting hurt, right?"
- "We didn't have this conversation."

Manager's Checklist for Chapter 1

❑ Be alert for the early signs of trouble so that you can take appropriate action to nip a budding problem.

❑ Analyze problems on their own terms. Avoid downplaying, distorting, or dismissing warning signs.

❑ Set realistic expectations for solving problems. Maintain a fair, balanced perspective so you avoid extreme optimism or pessimism.

❑ When evaluating a problem in its infancy, assess the odds of various outcomes. Predict what's highly likely, possible, and unlikely to occur.

❑ Ask yourself to what extent a brewing problem merits your attention or whether it'll go away without any action.

❑ Note three types of indications of trouble: abrupt changes in the way people communicate, sudden disruption of predictable patterns, and the hasty imposition of new, restrictive rules.

❑ Resist ethical lapses and insist on the same principled behavior from others. This lowers the odds that ethically questionable actions will lead to serious problems.

Profile of a Problem: The Six Stages

Throughout his military and diplomatic career, Secretary of State Colin Powell has managed thousands of people. His philosophy is to surround himself with talented, skillful staffers and give them the freedom to perform at their best.

At the same time, however, Powell wants to know about problems sooner rather than later. He tells his subordinates that alerting him of problems "isn't considered a sign of weakness or failure, but as a sign of mutual confidence." (*Investor's Business Daily*, May 27, 1999, p. A4)

Follow Powell's lead. Make it easy for employees to come to you with their concerns. If they sense something's wrong, you want to know about it. If they detect early signs of a production bottleneck, you want to help unclog it. If they make a costly error, show support and work with them to fix it so that they're not tempted to conceal the mistake.

Powell's management style works so well because it exposes problems in their infancy. After all, conflicts are rarely obvious from Day One. They tend to creep up on us. What starts as a minor mishap or an easy-to-ignore freak incident can soon spiral out of control and emerge as a far more serious issue. By pouncing on early signs of trouble, you give yourself the best chance to contain the fallout and plug relatively small holes before they swallow more time, money, and resources.

If you're rushing around putting out fires all day, it's understandable why you'd want to adopt a wait-and-see attitude with a problem—or simply refuse to think about it unless or until it grows in importance. After all, why fret or overreact if it might just go away?

Yet from my experience advising thousands of managers, I've found that problems tend to unfold in stages. They start small and gain both frequency and severity if left untended. I'll warn managers that unless they take a proactive approach (i.e., act now to investigate what's going on and confront the issue head on), they risk undergoing a potentially agonizing six-step process that prolongs the pain for everyone.

Stage 1: The Kindling Fire

Some ivory-tower consultants will urge you to see people problems as a blessing in disguise, a creative challenge that can double as a great team-building mechanism. They'll have you repeat lines like "Problems aren't a negative. They're a positive."

Don't believe a word of it.

In most cases, interpersonal conflicts start with simmering resentments. They intensify as pressures build and personalities clash. A manager who's going to survive under these conditions needs to intervene when people first show signs of getting on each other's nerves.

During the initial phase, a problem kindles like a fire warming up. Participants take sides and start to feel flashes of anger, indignation, and bitterness. But rather than communicate concerns or make amends in a straightforward manner, they might brush aside their annoyance or "suck it up" and move on.

That might strike your employees as the most sensible response, especially if they dread confrontation. But stewing in hostility tends to eat away at one's peace of mind. It becomes hard to concentrate on work if you're managing people who sit on opposite sides of the room in meetings and who start to form cliques of allies to gird for an us-against-them battle.

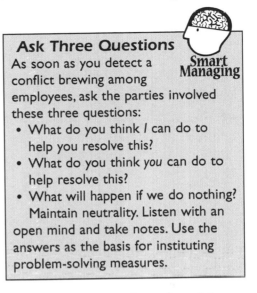

Ask Three Questions

As soon as you detect a conflict brewing among employees, ask the parties involved these three questions:

- What do you think *I* can do to help you resolve this?
- What do you think *you* can do to help resolve this?
- What will happen if we do nothing?

Maintain neutrality. Listen with an open mind and take notes. Use the answers as the basis for instituting problem-solving measures.

It's at this stage of the problem that you want to give employees a chance to vent and explain what's ailing them. Direct their frustration so that it doesn't feed on itself. Find a healthy outlet so everyone can stop stewing and start working toward solutions. Guide them to jump immediately to Stages 5 and 6—assessing the scope of the problem and taking action to resolve it.

Problems often fester when employees aren't sure what to do or whom to turn to. That's why you should build reserves of trust and support with everyone on your team. If individuals feel comfortable leveling with you about a problem as soon as it begins to nag at them, then you can get a head start on fixing it.

Yet some at-risk personalities will stoke a kindling fire. Rather than express their concerns about a problem and enlist your help, they'll hunker down and heat up inside. Here are some examples of personality types waiting to explode.

The grudge sponges. Some people just love to carry a grudge. They absorb each slight—perceived or real—as one more burden to bear. Rather than voice their objection, they'll stay silent, glower in fury, and, when asked, deny anything's wrong. Their favorite lines are *"I'm* not the problem" and "I'm just minding my own business."

The "right warriors." Perfectionists insist that everything they say or do is indisputably right. They believe themselves 100%

correct about everything. If coworkers disagree or even roll their eyes in doubt, former friends can turn into adversaries. Their favorite lines are "I know I'm right about this" and "There's no other explanation."

The wheel spinners. Hard-working self-starters are a pleasure to manage—unless they pride themselves on keeping so busy that they see themselves as heroic saviors. They may bury themselves in work, their desks strewn with piles of paper, only to resent everyone else for gabbing too much or taking too many breaks. Their favorite lines are "At least someone around here is working" and "I don't have time for that."

The oblivious ostriches. Like the big birds that habitually stick their heads in the sand, some employees will pretend everything's fine and look away from any unpleasantness. That's OK—to a point. But avoiding harsh reality only works temporarily. Eventually, it dawns on these individuals that they cannot turn away from problems forever. Their favorite lines are "Oh, that doesn't bother me at all" and "It doesn't matter to me."

If you recognize any of these personality types among your employees, make an extra effort to keep open lines of communication with them. Be friendly and accessible and you'll probably hear about problems before they grow.

Stage 2: The Close Brush with Doom

Given enough time, problems will eventually rear their ugly heads. An argument will erupt between team leaders. An internal miscommunication will result in a wasted opportunity. Misapplication of a rule or regulation will alienate and nearly drive away a key customer.

In most cases, the first flare-up of a problem won't do lasting harm. But like two airplanes that come within a few hundred yards of a collision, a near-miss disaster can offer an invaluable learning experience.

Here's when your role changes from manager to student. You must adopt the perspective of someone who's curious about a problem, who's studying it and trying to learn from it. You want to dissect a problem and identify ways to stamp it out in the future.

Sadly, some managers act more like know-it-all teachers than open-minded students. They put undue pressure on themselves to have all the answers, all the time. They focus on dishing out orders and explanations for a potentially costly blunder, rather than stepping back and learning from it.

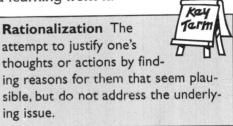

Resist the urge to rationalize every problem. Just because you can reassure yourself (or your boss) that an argument between two of your employees was a "one-

> **Rationalization** The attempt to justify one's thoughts or actions by finding reasons for them that seem plausible, but do not address the underlying issue.

time event that'll never happen again," you're still not in the clear. You need to talk with both combatants, hear both sides, develop strategies for them to get along, and get them to agree to work together more harmoniously from now on.

Your response to a near-miss disaster largely depends on whether you're personally involved or a spectator. If you're managing a problem from a distance, it's easier to learn from it dispassionately. Through observation and evaluation, you can come away with lessons that you can apply to prevent further problems.

If you're directly engaged in the problem, however, detaching yourself is tougher. Protecting your ego or reputation can complicate your effort to review the situation objectively. You might want to hide your misjudgment or miscalculation from higher-ups, leading you to deny responsibility for your actions or decisions.

At this stage of a problem—after it has kindled for a while and then showed signs of flaming up—you need to sweep away mental clutter so that you can promptly extinguish the fire. Otherwise, it's likely to spread and lead to more dire consequences.

How can you clear your head to learn from a close brush

with doom? Here's a five-step process that helps cleanse your mind so that you can learn the right lessons.

After you experience a near disaster, don't heave a sigh of relief that it's not worse and convince yourself the problem will never recur. Instead, strive to learn from it. Here's how:

1. Close your eyes. Breathe deeply for 30 seconds.
2. Imagine you're resting in a calm, pleasing place, such as a private beach or a mountain peak. Arouse your senses so that you see, smell, hear, and touch the beauty and serenity around you. Make it as real as possible in your head.
3. Visualize those individuals who played a role in the problem. Allow them to enter your idyllic environment. See only their physical characteristics; don't let your judgments interfere.
4. Visualize the problem as an object, such as a boat or beach ball. See the people and the problem independently from each other.
5. Pretend you join with the people involved to push the problem away (i.e., throwing the ball far into the sea). Then see yourself laughing with them about how you rid yourselves of the problem and what you learned.

Visualization works well because it lets you depersonalize the problem. You extract the right lessons from the outset because you're analyzing events in an unbiased frame of mind. This approach enables you to make connections and expose underlying tensions that you might otherwise miss.

Consider the case of Tammy, a marketing manager I coached recently. As we were wrapping up a meeting, she mentioned as an aside that she almost lost her job but "it all blew over." Surprised by her casual tone, I asked her to tell me more. Tammy explained that for the last few months a freelance photographer she hired for photo shoots was missing deadlines by a few days and not following directions. This struck her as a minor annoyance but she let it slide. I recognized this as Stage 1, the kindling phase of a problem.

Then near disaster struck. The photographer failed to show for a critical job. Tammy had spared no expense to rent a beautiful loft for this photo shoot. She had prepared the elaborate scene so it was perfect. The company president had dropped by to watch.

But no one could reach the missing photographer. As each minute ticked by, the president's mood darkened and it appeared the company might wind up wasting thousands of dollars. Luckily, Tammy knew another photographer with a nearby studio. She called and he agreed to race over and help.

After hearing Tammy's story, I told her this was a classic Stage 2 event—a close brush with doom. She had intended to chastise the photographer for not showing up and use him less. I urged her to take away more lessons from the mishap and plot how to prevent problems later on. Together we practiced how she would communicate her concerns with the photographer and possibly terminate their contract for good. We also listed contingencies she'd take to avoid similar problems on future photo shoots.

Learn from Tammy's messy experience. If a problem almost costs you your job but it "blows over," take it to heart. Treat it as a warning to respond the next time in a more effective manner.

Trust me: there *will* be a next time. Prepare for it.

Stage 3: Multiple Outbreaks

In an ideal world, managers would solve problems as soon as they surfaced. They would recognize the clues early on and take decisive action. If a near disaster occurred, they would drop whatever else they were doing to address the threat of further mishaps.

Yet here's what actually happens all too often: A manager reacts to a brush with doom by saying, "Phew! That was close. Am I lucky!" The manager then makes a few cosmetic or half-hearted attempts to deal with the problem and promptly forgets about it.

A few uneventful days—or weeks—pass. The manager no longer focuses on the problem. But, of course, it doesn't disappear. It lingers. Evidence accrues that it's spreading. Instead of another close call, the problem rears its head in other, more subtle ways. Examples:

- A once-reliable employee arrives late to make a critical presentation to a client. You salvage the account, but in the following weeks this employee falls behind on routine paperwork, files a grievance with Human Resources about the company's vacation policy, and no longer makes follow-up calls to customers to ensure their satisfaction.
- Your star salesperson tries to quit, but you make a lavish counteroffer and she decides to stay. But in the following weeks, two other high-performing salespeople request time off and a sales manager scales back his duties. Before you know it, you've got a decimated sales force.
- You discover you've entered the wrong data on a financial exhibit that's part of a major report to your CEO. Had you not caught it just in time, the CEO would've drawn the wrong conclusion and possibly initiated layoffs. But in the following weeks, your employees point out other errors you've made in your computations and your outside accounting firm questions your figures in yet another report.

In the above cases, a potentially huge debacle is averted. But the problem resurfaces later in less dire but still significant ways. This pattern replays itself frequently when managers do not quash problems once and for all when they first appear.

Stage 4: Blaming, Denying, and Sniping

This stage can get ugly.

Once enough evidence accumulates that you've got a real problem on your hands, you might instinctively lash out at yourself or others for allowing the situation to escalate to this point. You can no longer deny the mess you're in. And you can

Keep a Cheat Sheet

After you skirt a near disaster, take a sheet of paper and write the problem that you faced across the top of the page. Example:

Problem: I entered the wrong data on a financial exhibit prepared for CEO.

Leave the rest of the sheet blank. Post it in a private place where you'll see it every day.

If a similar problem arises, write it down on the sheet. Include even the most minor mishaps on your log. Example:

- Jim noticed I miscalculated our monthly administrative expenses.
- Sandy fixed my spreadsheet so that it didn't count product returns twice.
- Our accountants told me I didn't give enough detail of our equipment purchases last quarter.

Keeping a written record of subsequent problems provides stark evidence that something's amiss. You'll find it harder to ignore these multiple outbreaks if you force yourself to list each one.

no longer cling to the belief that you survived a one-time flare-up that won't recur.

You're angry, bitter, and frustrated. You want to throw a fit, assign the blame, and justify your actions. Worst of all, you know your reputation as a manager has taken a hit. You've lost credibility and demonstrated to one and all that you're ill equipped to solve problems quickly or efficiently.

With the benefit of hindsight, you know deep down you handled things poorly. You missed the signs of trouble brewing (Stage 1). You waved off a near disaster as a freak occurrence (Stage 2). You watched as multiple outbreaks spread (Stage 3). And now it's obvious you must engage fully and take charge of a solution.

But first you need to vent.

In Stage 4, actual problem solving takes a back seat as you cover your tracks, point fingers, and undercut the role others played in trying to help. You take responsibility only to a limited degree—and seek to defend your actions up to this point.

As you read this, you may be thinking, "Oh, I'm not like

Enron's End Run

Throughout the summer and fall of 2001, before Enron Corp. acknowledged massive losses and filed for the biggest bankruptcy in U.S. history, its senior executives were stuck in Stage 4. They publicly denied any problem existed, even while they dumped their Enron stock. They ignored—and in some cases castigated—a vice president for writing a memo that criticized the company's fraudulent accounting. The CEO, Jeffrey Skilling, resigned suddenly just three months before the bankruptcy filing. Instead of confronting the core problem—that key executives had created literally thousands of partnerships to hide losses from investors—the top brass resorted to blaming their "loose cannon" managers and outside accountants, denying their involvement, and sniping at the press, legislators, and government regulators.

that. If I allowed a problem to get out of control, I'd admit it and do my best to deal with it."

That's an admirable response. But in the heat of the moment, with top executives watching your every move with a disapproving glare, you might react differently. Why come clean if you can blame others? That doesn't make you a weak or defective manager; it just shows you're human.

If you're managing an employee who's blaming, denying, and sniping, it rarely works to issue a "Stop that!" command. Try listening—to a point—and then saying, "It's more important that we solve the problem." Shift the employee's emphasis from looking back to looking forward.

Stage 5: Acknowledging the Scope

Ah, you've made it. You've worked through your demons and you're finally ready to think like a problem-solver. Feels good, doesn't it?

Now it's time to wrap your mind around the *whole* problem, to consider it from every angle so that you can appreciate its scope. You don't just dwell on a narrow issue with which you're most comfortable; you evaluate a multifaceted conflict in all its glory.

> ### Ward Off Selective Listening
> **CAUTION!**
>
> When you're ready to confront a conflict, watch out if you start saying to peers or employees, "I don't want to hear about that now" or "We'll worry about that later" or branding someone a "malcontent" for raising another, related problem. Be a sponge. Listen to everything your colleagues say about the problem, even if what you hear complicates matters or introduces issues you hadn't identified. Don't fall into the trap of brushing aside such comments and selectively listening to remarks that either confirm what you already know or validate your plan of attack.

To ensure that you acknowledge the full scope of a problem, assess it on many levels:

- **The history to date.** Study what has happened so far. Like a historian, start at the beginning and trace the sequence of events that has led to where you are now. Write a summary of how the problem arose, what factors influenced its development, and where it stands today.
- **The stakes.** Define what's at risk, whether it's money, personnel, or the company's reputation. This helps you and your staff appreciate the urgency of solving the problem. It can also serve as a motivational tool as you prepare to mobilize your team to do what's needed to reach a solution.
- **The unknowns.** Most problems come with variables—the tricky unknowns that can affect the outcome. Work with your colleagues to list all the gray areas that come into play, such as the possibility of reorganizing your department or pending litigation that might affect your staff's ability to meet certain deadlines.
- **The line between what you can and cannot control.** Acknowledge what falls outside your sphere of influence. Accept that no matter what solution steps you take, challenges can crop up that it's impossible to predict or plan for. By evaluating what's within your control, you gain the power to solve whatever you can while monitoring forces beyond your grasp.

Among the most important questions to ask as you digest a problem is "How does it affect ____?" Fill in the blank by plugging in every conceivable ingredient of your business (e.g., my employees, my coworkers, my bosses, my clients or customers, my time management, my priorities, my goals, my budget, my flexibility, my attitude, next week's meeting, our bottom line).

Evaluating the potential influence of a problem on many levels helps you appreciate its scope. It also motivates you to muster the energy and will to combat and conquer it.

Stage 6: Mobilizing Action

Now, it's time to act!

Once you dissect a problem and study all its repercussions, you're ready to plot an action plan. You know what you're up against. Now, you need a systematic way to solve it.

You're accountable for fixing what's broken in your unit, but that doesn't mean you must fly solo. Involve your staff in the problem-solving process. Explain the situation and why it merits immediate attention. Present a menu of possible action steps and ask for their input.

While it's wise to turn to your employees for help, don't equate group problem solving with an exercise in democracy. The buck stops with you. Staffers should lend their opinions and voice concerns and objections, but they don't have a formal vote in what actions you ultimately take. Everyone need not sign off on your solution.

"People don't demand votes on each and every issue, but they generally want to be heard regarding the diagnosis of the current situation and/or the potential cures," says Jean-Francois Manzoni, associate professor at INSEAD in Fontainebleau, France (*Harvard Management Update*, February 2002, p. 7).

At this stage, adopt what consultant Tom Peters calls "a bias for action." Run experiments, test your theories, and assign project teams to implement solutions. Reinforce the need for everyone to make headway or at least learn what will and will not work in treating the problem.

As you plunge into action, create a mechanism for monitoring your progress. Know in advance how you'll measure your success. I find that technically oriented managers like to use a spreadsheet or matrix to track actions and results. Less scientific types may prefer to set

> ### Easy as 1, 2, 3
>
> Savvy managers can collect the best problem-solving ideas from employees with a simple tool: a piece of paper. Take a blank sheet, write 1, 2 and 3 along the left margin, make photocopies and give one to each member of your team. Say, "I'd like you to list the top three actions you think we can take to address this problem."

quantitative and qualitative objectives and see if they're meeting them within a set time frame. The key is to develop a score-keeping method so that you know at a glance whether the actions you take produce the results you want.

Manager's Checklist for Chapter 2

- ❏ Encourage employees to share their concerns with you. Don't shoot the messenger.

- ❏ When you detect a problem brewing, don't automatically adopt a wait-and-see attitude. When you notice employees stewing in anger, encourage them to open up to you.

- ❏ After you experience a near disaster in your unit, investigate so that it doesn't recur. Don't rationalize it as a one-time event.

- ❏ Keep a log of every instance in which a problem resurfaces. That makes it harder to ignore multiple outbreaks.

- ❏ If employees resort to blaming, denying, or sniping, redirect their focus on looking forward—not backward—and solving the problem.

- ❏ To appreciate the scope of a problem, analyze its history, the stakes, the unknowns, and what you can and cannot control.

- ❏ Engage your employees in devising action steps. Solicit their best ideas and work with them to track your progress.

Jumping from Problem to Solution

Paul loved to talk about his problems at work. He'd call me a few times a week to review everything going wrong: late deliveries, poor communication among his staff, sloppy reporting procedures in his department, his "inaccessible and inscrutable" boss, budgetary pressures, and demanding clients.

As his coach, I'd indulge him—to a point. Just talking through all these tough issues seemed therapeutic for him. But after 15 or 20 minutes of detailing all his problems, he still didn't seem any closer to figuring out what to do next.

That's when I started to ask him, "What would you rather spend time on today: listing all your problems or making progress on one of them?"

Paul started to dice his troubles into manageable bits. He'd isolate what bothered him the most and skip right to solution steps. Within minutes, he'd go from an exasperated worrywart to an empowered, forward-thinking leader. He perked up when we batted around ideas to mitigate damage, change others' undesirable behavior, and reform internal processes to gain efficiency.

When you're immersed in problems, they tend to take on a life all their own. You can't believe how everything's haywire. So you talk about it, talk some more, and then repeat. It's a time-consuming and ultimately futile cycle.

A better approach involves action planning. You focus less on the number of difficulties you face and more on what must happen for each one to go away. You look ahead with optimism rather than look back with regret. You treat time as a precious resource and use every minute to advance toward solutions. That's the kind of sensible, no-nonsense mindset you need to survive the rigors of management.

Four Steps to the Promised Land

You need a system to solve problems. By applying the same formula consistently to treat each obstacle you face, you gain confidence and muster the strength to graduate from words to action. Like Paul, the best managers eventually learn to apportion their time wisely and not gab too much about their problems without doing anything to fix them.

Here's a four-step process that speeds your progression from problem to solution. Ideally, you should move rapidly from stage to stage without dallying or second-guessing. As you master this process, you'll find the steps blend together seamlessly. It takes practice, but within a few months you should save time and make faster headway in conquering the on-the-job challenges you face.

1. Identify Your Options

Rookie managers tend to latch onto the first solution that enters their mind. Rather than weigh alternatives fairly, they might reshape a problem in their head to make it fit their preconceived notion of what they want to do next.

You may think that if you're sure you know what to do to put out a fire, you should do it—pronto. And it's a safe bet your first action plan may work just fine. But there's a danger of moving *too* fast: You might overlook smarter, bolder, more creative solutions.

> **⚠ CAUTION!**
>
> ### Anchors Away!
> The order in which you think of solutions can influence which one you prefer. It's common to embrace the first set of information that pops into mind at the expense of ideas, options, or compelling data that seep in later. Unduly favoring what you think of first is called *anchoring* or *hindsight bias*. Once you're anchored to a strand of information or action, it distorts your ability to consider alternatives or process additional data.
>
> By casting anchors aside and not fixating on the initial solution that jumps into your mind, you increase the odds of identifying the best course of action.

At the opposite extreme, you must avoid talking your problem to death. Engaging in woe-is-me whining or storming around in a disgusted daze also won't help you race toward a solution. As we'll learn in Chapter 5, controlling your emotions saves enormous time and allows you to bounce back quickly with the least amount of pain.

In coming up with lots of options on how to reach a solution, free your mind to work at its best. How? Express a problem as a question. In a calm, unhurried moment, let your subconscious run wild as you answer it.

Consider how Colleen, a manager at an e-commerce firm, dealt with a mounting backlog of customer orders. We worked together on reframing her problem as a question: How can I eliminate the backlog of orders? Then she listed alternatives for solutions over the next few days. Colleen decided to keep a tape recorder by her bed and activate it whenever she wanted to add another idea to the mix.

"I'm least distracted by stuff right before I go to bed and right when I wake up," she said. "That's when I think the most clearly." But she didn't want to forget her brainstorms, so she made sure her tape recorder was within easy reach. She wound up with seven viable options for eliminating the backlog and improving her unit's operating efficiency.

If you're indecisive and you dread making choices, you may find this step especially vexing. Don't shortchange yourself.

Produce a lengthy list of possible problem-solving moves, even if some of the entries strike you at first as too costly or off the wall.

2. Grade Your Ideas

Once you've generated at least three—and preferably more— solid options, shift gears. Remove your quantity hat and think quality. Which alternatives offer the most promise? Which ones stand the greatest chance of achieving quick, low-risk success? Do any options overlap? What additional information do you need to determine if certain alternatives are feasible?

As you evaluate your alternatives, measure them consistently. Remove your blinders to give each option a fair hearing. In your eagerness to take action, you might rush through your choices and pick the one that's easiest, safest, or most appealing to your bosses or employees. But that defeats the purpose of the process. It's vital to apply a comprehensive measuring system to each option so that you weigh them properly.

If you're a teacher at heart, you may want to assign a grade to each option. Avoid letter grades. With an A-to-F system, you'll find yourself doling out low As, Bs, and Cs to almost every idea. Give yourself more flexibility and accuracy by using a 1-to-100 scale with 100 as best. Assign a number to a series of measurable criteria such as:

- Level of control you'll exert over outcome

The Index Card Test

Here's a low-tech way to grade each of your problem-solving options. Take a pile of blank index cards. Write each option across the top of a card on *both sides*. Then, on one side only, draw two columns with the headings **Pro** and **Con**. List all the advantages and disadvantages that you associate with each idea. When you're finished, put the card aside until the next morning (if time permits). Then add any new pros and cons that come to mind. Now *turn the cards over* and give them to a colleague whom you respect and admire. Ask that person to list pros and cons of each problem you wrote at the top of the card. Compare both analyses and you'll have an excellent sense of each option's plusses and minuses.

- Likelihood of achieving desired outcome
- Cost of implementation
- Readiness to implement
- Receptivity of colleagues and staff to the proposed solution

By setting up specific criteria to grade each option, you create a sound template for judging your solutions. This adds to the transparency and reliability of the process.

3. Choose and Commit

Now you're ready to choose the most promising action plan and gain the support to make it work. If you've graded your alternatives with care, the best solution often becomes self-evident.

A claims manager at an insurance company told me how he identified five options for addressing a problem with his field adjusters' unacceptably slow rate of closing files. He graded each one of his five choices on a 1-to-100 scale and wound up with results of 44, 49, 60, 68, and 88. The highest-scoring option also ranked highest in his boss's view, so everything fell together and he knew he'd found the most attractive solution without fretting about making the wrong choice.

That's how it's supposed to work.

Yet the process stalls if you choose an option but don't commit to it. That's a surprisingly common mistake managers make. If you're too risk-averse, for instance, you might make a half-hearted attempt to implement a solution but stop midstream before you can effectively evaluate your progress. Or you might announce that you've arrived at an action plan to address a problem and then let yourself be swayed by naysayers or diverted by new priorities.

Key Term Conditional commitment Decision to take a specific action only in certain circumstances. Example: I'll adopt that strategy *if* sales continue to dip next month. Setting too many conditions (or "if" statements) on your commitment limits your agility in responding to problems.

At this stage of the problem-solving process, it helps to visualize the act of triumphantly passing the point of no return. Examples of scenes in which you make a choice and commit to it can range from seeing yourself jump off a diving board into a swimming pool to signing your name to a contract to buy a house. By conjuring up such images, you reinforce your intention to take decisive action and give it your full effort.

Another way to seal your commitment is to tell someone what you're about to do. Let a coworker know how you intend to solve a problem and what steps you're going to take. Explaining your course of action to others raises your accountability. It also enables you to collect last-minute feedback so that you can adjust and finalize your plan before you implement it.

4. Execute for Results

When you know you've chosen the best solution, it makes successful follow-through seem almost preordained. You have faith in yourself to follow your plan. As obstacles arise, you can swat them away with confidence. You may conclude that other choices would've worked just as well, but you're certain the strategy you're pursuing makes the most sense. As a result, you do everything in your power to make it work.

The first three steps listed above—listing options, grading them, and choosing the best one—may sound laborious. But you'll soon find you can speed through them in an hour or so. It's only when you reach the final stage of execution that procrastination threatens to derail you. Some managers assume the hard work's behind them. Now that they know what to do, they foolishly allow themselves to relax.

"It felt like I had already solved the problem," said Brady, a manager whom I trained to adopt this problem-solving process. Yet he had only completed steps one through three at that point. "I figured I had thought through the situation and come up with the right plan of attack. The rest seemed so easy now."

Letting up at this stage can wreak havoc. Unless you're truly pinched for time, you might give yourself permission to shelve the problem for a while and shift your attention to other matters. It's surprisingly common for managers to convince themselves

TRICKS OF THE TRADE

Apply the "Three to Five" Rule

To ward off procrastination when you're set to implement a solution, use what Jeffrey Davidson, author of *10 Minute Guide to Managing Your Time* (New York: Macmillan, 2000), calls the "three to five method." Think of three to five actions you can take right away to advance toward a solution. This can include preparatory steps—or "easy entry" activities—that soften your resistance for plunging head-long into solving the problem. Examples include calling individuals whom you're going to enlist to help you (and leaving messages if they're not in), creating new files you'll need to categorize your findings, or developing a questionnaire you'll use to measure customer satisfaction in addressing the problem. Taking these initial action steps will give you the momentum to charge ahead without further delay.

they're home free because they've arrived at a practical, realistic solution. Executing may seem anticlimactic!

Some managers confess to me that, despite their diligent effort to weigh their options and pick the best solution, they feel reluctant to follow through. They may sigh and say, "I'm having second thoughts about all this" or "There are so many related problems beyond this to deal with."

I'm not a psychologist, but after hearing this enough times I'm convinced a part of them fears success and dreads having to find out if they really possess the necessary skills and determination to stamp out a tough problem.

The true test of your management prowess is your ability to fix what's broken. That means diagnosing the problem, choosing the appropriate solution, and then getting "under the hood" to make dirty and often complicated repairs.

Remember that your boss will judge you first and foremost on how you execute. If you're going to thrive in your job and ascend to the next level, let nothing stand in the way when it's time to implement your problem-solving plan.

Acting vs. Stewing

Jumping from problem to solution requires planning and acting. It shouldn't get bogged down in aimless chatter. But it often does.

When you first confront a problem, talking it out can help. Analyzing the situation with colleagues and sharing ideas on what to do next often brings people together and ensures everyone's aiming at the right goal. It also allows you to gather insights from others so that you base your decisions on a broad range of input.

The downside of all this discussion is that your team may talk too much and do too little. Your peers and employees might tell you why the problem's worse than you think, what won't work to treat it, what related dangers lurk in the background, and what mistakes were made in the past that led to this sorry state of affairs.

It amazes me how employees come alive when a big problem blows into town. They gesture with more force and animation. They stop mumbling and start speaking up. They have a glimmer in their eyes, as if something's happening around them that's special and exciting. Don't be surprised if your previously listless and apathetic crew suddenly seems infused with energy in the early stages of a crisis.

In some cases, *you* might be the one who's stewing or living in the past—not your employees. Beware of spending too much time chastising yourself for yesterday's blunders and telling anyone who'll listen that you should've known better. In the midst of

> ⚠ CAUTION!
>
> ### Past, Present, Future
> You know you're in trouble when you and your staff hash out a problem by dwelling on the past rather than studying the present or looking ahead. Too much reflection can lead to regret and recriminations. Bickering can ensue as individuals try to defend past actions or justify decisions that, in retrospect, now seem faulty. To make sure your team solves problems rather than succumbs to them, limit the amount of time they focus on the past. Use props: bring a rearview mirror from a car or a crystal ball (or fortune cookies) to a staff meeting. Whenever people start harping on what's already happened and what's too late to change, hold up the rearview mirror as a silent reminder for them to stop looking back. Or point to the crystal ball to redirect their focus on the future.

a serious problem, no one wants to hear you berate yourself. They want you to lead.

Seeking Wise Counsel

In your eagerness to plunge into solutions, don't tune out the guidance that others try to provide.

Collecting the best ideas of those around you sounds obvious. Managers usually assure me, "I know I don't have all the answers. I always find out what others think." That's easy enough to say. But the real test is how hard they try to gather input, whom they seek out, and what they do with the information they get.

Like any skill, asking for advice takes practice. Your tone, choice of words, and demeanor must strike just the right chord in order to induce others to open up and provide thoughtful, clearheaded insight. If you start by poking your head sheepishly into someone's office and apologizing for bothering them, you're already fighting an uphill battle. They'll see you as weak and lacking assertiveness, so they may act condescending rather than supportive.

When an urgent problem arises, you and your team may lack the luxury of time. Instead of soliciting advice from mentors, you might latch onto whatever flavor-of-the-month tip you stumble across in a magazine article or inflate the importance of a comment supposedly made by the CEO that's been passed along to you. That's not an especially effective way to gain the wisdom you need to handle your problems.

Even when you're under time pressure, allot at least an hour or two to bounce your ideas off a mentor or trusted friend. Present the problem succinctly and see how he or she responds. The simple act of "talking out" the situation can in itself prove therapeutic.

Solicit advice from a cross section of individuals both inside and outside your organization. Discuss the problem with a boss and coworker who have experience dealing with similar challenges. Also consider seeking out someone whom you admire in

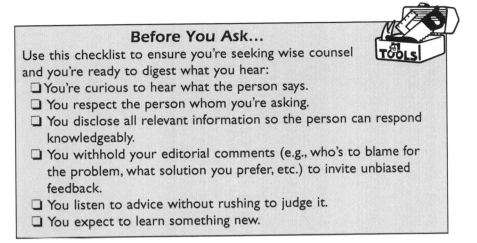

Before You Ask...
Use this checklist to ensure you're seeking wise counsel
and you're ready to digest what you hear:
- ❑ You're curious to hear what the person says.
- ❑ You respect the person whom you're asking.
- ❑ You disclose all relevant information so the person can respond knowledgeably.
- ❑ You withhold your editorial comments (e.g., who's to blame for the problem, what solution you prefer, etc.) to invite unbiased feedback.
- ❑ You listen to advice without rushing to judge it.
- ❑ You expect to learn something new.

another industry, such as a friend or a former colleague.
Executive coaches come in handy. Also contact the author of
your favorite business book (like me!) and editors of management publications. They often respond to subscribers' questions.

As editor of *Working Smart* newsletter, I often received calls
and e-mails from readers in search of input. I would ask them to
summarize their problem, list its causes, and share any solutions that they were weighing. I'd ask clarifying questions, collect more information as needed, and give my opinion on what
actions they could take. If you or your company subscribes to
newsletters or belongs to professional associations, it's worth a
call to see if they provide experts on call for quick counseling.

When sharing your problem with others, brace yourself to
hear what you don't want to hear. Managers often fall into the
trap of either neglecting sound advice or twisting it around so
that it reinforces what they want to do anyway. Beware of the
following pitfalls.

Shutting down. If someone tells you something objectionable,
you might dismiss it outright, refuse to listen, or interrupt to
declare certain topics off-limits. Train yourself to absorb even
the most outlandish or upsetting advice. Evaluate it only when
you're thinking clearly and free of swirling emotions.

Paying lip service. Some managers react enthusiastically at first to wise counsel but then fail to apply it. Their initial burst of excitement doesn't translate into action. If you're going to hunt for solutions, prepare to pounce on them when they're presented to you. Otherwise, others may realize you're unwilling to take responsibility for solving problems and they'll hesitate to help you in the future.

Filtering out the harsh truth. Some problems require acting in ways that you dread. So you focus on one aspect of a mentor's advice—the part that you agree with—while disregarding everything else.

Asking for help only pays off if you keep an open mind. Listen to your intuition. But balance your gut instinct (and whatever problem-solving approach you prefer) with the insights you glean from others. Give them a fair hearing so that you collect the best ideas they have to offer.

Generating Group Buy-In

When you shift into problem-solving mode, you can't operate in a vacuum. Your employees and colleagues inevitably play a role.

Ideally, your associates should help you craft a solution. Make them feel like participants, not spectators, and they'll support your efforts wholeheartedly. Share your concerns, solicit their feedback, and exchange ideas on what to do next. If they ask smart questions, either have them research the answers or do so yourself. Show that you're eager to involve them at every step along the way until the solution's up and running.

The same rules apply even if you don't necessarily need your coworkers to help you implement the solution. They should still feel a sense of shared interest in combating the problem; that's one of the ways to foster teamwork and create camaraderie in a diverse workforce. You let your peers and employees off the hook if you internalize everything so that all the pressures rest on your shoulders.

To gain their buy-in, let them know what's wrong, why it matters, and what actions you're taking (hopefully with their approval) to address it. Ask for their suggestions even if you don't expect much in return. Taking the trouble to explain what's going on and what you're doing about it—and inviting them to chime in on how to proceed—serves a valuable purpose in itself.

> ### Sharing the Problem
> When Bob Pike, a renowned speaker and trainer, finds his presentation time cut at the last minute and can no longer cover all 10 points as planned, he lets the group in on his dilemma and enlists their help. He starts by saying he has time to cover only five of his 10 points. He lists the 10 on a flip chart and asks the group to select their "top five." Then, he discusses the five topics with the most votes.

To earn everyone's blessing, you might be tempted either to undersell the problem or oversell your solution. That's a mistake. Characterize the problem in stark, honest terms. Highlight the risks of both action and inaction, along with how the problem might affect your peers and employees over the short and long haul. Admit what you don't know. Mention your fears or concerns.

Recall how President George W. Bush responded to the attacks of September 11, 2001. He repeatedly emphasized that it would take years of determined action to rid the world of terrorist cells, that there was no quick fix, that the battle would extract a toll on Americans and require considerable sacrifice. For the most part, he resisted the urge to underplay the problem or present an overly optimistic timetable for resolving it. Many pundits concluded that his levelheaded appraisal of the situation convinced Americans to support him in the months following the attacks as he sent U.S. troops to war.

You take a journey whenever you attempt to solve a problem. Surprises and disappointments await you. Foul-ups can add to your troubles. Luck—and fate—can work for or against you. But no matter how events unfold, you'll want the members of your team by your side. And the best way to earn their support is to give them a voice and involve them every step of the way.

Manager's Checklist for Chapter 3

❏ Dice your problems into manageable bits and then deal with them, one by one. Don't waste too much time talking about them without *doing* anything.

❏ To solve a problem: list all possible solutions, grade them, commit to the best course of action, and follow through.

❏ Confront challenges by looking ahead to what you must do to address them. Every minute you berate yourself for past blunders is one less minute you can devote to solving them.

❏ Spend an hour or two talking out your ideas with a trusted ally.

❏ When you ask for advice, prepare to hear what you don't want to hear. Listen with an open mind.

❏ Involve your team—peers and employees—in your problem solving. Discuss your concerns, solicit their feedback, and exchange ideas on how to proceed.

Preventing Misunderstandings

If you analyzed each of the problems you faced in a typical month, well over half of them would probably result at least in part from a communication breakdown. In the rush of workaday pressures, it's almost impossible to ensure that every message you send and receive gets transmitted with full accuracy.

Misunderstandings produce a destructive ripple effect. Even if you pounce on a problem early and eliminate the source of confusion, ill will can remain. Employees may resent wasting their time and energy on unnecessary tasks. Vendors may feel embarrassed that they acted based on the wrong information. Your boss may conclude you're an unreliable source and no longer trust you.

While you'll never rid yourself of misunderstandings, you can take steps to lower the odds that they'll occur. Listen without bias. Confirm what you hear. Ask clarifying questions. Prioritize what you say by putting the most important information up front. Withhold your judgments.

A manager who wants to communicate better can start by

treating each message as a code to crack. The words themselves are your first clue. But you also want to consider the speaker's body language, vocal patterns, and record. Someone who has a history of sowing confusion or leaving you falsely reassured may do so again. That's when you need to take extra care to overcome obstacles and capture the true message.

Listening to Learn

The primary cause of miscommunication is poor listening. In exercising authority over staff, managers often focus on what they say and how they say it. By choosing the right words, speaking in a forceful tone, and repeating key points, they figure they'll make themselves heard. But the more they focus on sending messages, the less they care about receiving them. To reduce misunderstandings, devote as much attention to listening as speaking. Here are some steps to boost your concentration.

Explore, then exclaim. Use questions to advance a conversation. Withhold your statements until after you've given others ample time to talk and you've learned what's on their minds. Otherwise, you risk talking yourself into a corner.

Carole, a supervisor at an assembly plant, complained to me that she kept "crossing wires" with her workers. She would tell them how to operate certain machines and check for defects. But they would "never seem to get it right," she said in exasperation. When I observed her on the job, the problem was obvious: Carole never stopped talking. She would bark orders and reminders constantly, rarely letting her workers respond. So we agreed she would ask more questions and make fewer statements. Instead of saying, "Tim, remember that you have to check the filter," she'd ask, "Tim, did you check the filter?" Sure enough, Carole's employees began to understand her better. The more she listened to them, the sooner she was able to identify potential misunderstandings and communicate in a calm, reassuring manner.

Give the extra-second gift. The simplest way to avoid costly misunderstandings is to wait an extra second before you respond. Mentally count to two. If the other person appears attentive and has nothing to add, take that as your signal to speak.

In your eagerness to talk, you might chime in at your earliest opportunity. That leads to talking over others and blurting out your opinions or instructions too soon.

This creates a double risk. In your haste to speak, you may miss the point the speaker was trying to make and you'll probably convince the speaker that you weren't listening—that you were merely planning your reply the whole time while waiting impatiently to break in and talk. Later in this chapter, we discuss interrupting in more detail.

Make the pieces fit. When you do a jigsaw puzzle, you can't force pieces to fit that don't match. The same goes for conversations. Listen so that you make sense of what you hear. If something's confusing or contradictory, don't shrug it off and force it to fit into what you already believe. Stay attuned to the speaker, ask questions, and root out inconsistencies.

Harried managers often jump to conclusions. Misunderstandings result when they assume they know what someone's trying to say, so they act on incomplete or incorrect information.

Stop the daydreaming! Most of us can listen to about 600 words a minute. The normal rate of speech is about 125 to 150 words a minute. That means we need to devote only limited attention to what others say in order to capture the meaning.

It's tempting to waste all that extra mental capacity. Thinking of your weekend plans or your love life while an employee warns you about a technical glitch almost guarantees further problems later. It's better to harness all your energy to observe the speaker's nonverbal behavior, consider your history of interaction with this person, and consider what questions you want to ask.

Ask Permission First

Give yourself permission to daydream. That's better than letting your mind wander freely. The next time you're struggling to concentrate on a speaker, ask yourself, "Do I understand everything that's being said?" or "Am I paying full attention?" Only after you're sure you can answer "yes" should you consider allowing yourself to take a mental stroll and partially tune out. Giving yourself permission to daydream prevents you from automatically wandering too far from the conversation and missing key information.

Where's Your Receipt?

When you buy groceries at the market, you get a receipt. It confirms that you paid for the items you purchased.

When you listen accurately to a speaker, you don't get a printed receipt. Too bad. Countless misunderstandings would be averted if we received confirmation that we've understood a speaker's point in its entirety.

Checking with a speaker to confirm you understand the message is like getting a receipt. When you're both acknowledging each other's points, you create rapport and tie together loose ends of the conversation. You may not agree on everything, but at least you attain mutual understanding. And that will insulate both of you from explosive problems.

Paraphrasing what you hear lowers the risk of misunderstanding. Get into the habit of restating a point succinctly or asking for clarification even when you're fairly sure you got the point the first time. Wait for the other person's go-ahead before you draw conclusions. This is the next best thing to getting a receipt in return for your listening.

Paraphrasing doesn't come naturally to many people. Yet the most effective communicators train themselves to review what's been said before they go ahead. If you manage staff, stopping to summarize what someone said may seem time-consuming and unnecessary—until you realize how many misunderstandings might otherwise result.

In one of my seminars, I was explaining the importance of paraphrasing to a group of health care professionals. I could see some of them rolling their eyes. They were probably thinking, "Oh, come on! Every minute counts in my job. The last thing I have time for is going over what every patient says."

Fortunately, a nurse spoke up.

"What you're saying reminds me of how I was trained to give an intra-

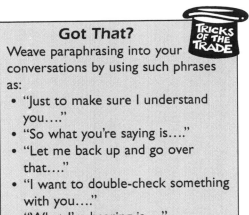

Got That?

Weave paraphrasing into your conversations by using such phrases as:

- "Just to make sure I understand you...."
- "So what you're saying is...."
- "Let me back up and go over that...."
- "I want to double-check something with you...."
- "What I'm hearing is...."

muscular injection," she said. "When we insert the needle, we're trained to pull back on the syringe slightly to check for blood. As long as there's no blood in the syringe, we can proceed with the shot."

Granted, that's not the most pleasant image. But it helps if you can visualize in some way the act of looping back before you skip ahead. Taking a "one step back, two steps forward" approach protects you from drawing the wrong conclusion or racing headfirst into costly problems.

Culprits of the Mind

Like your immune system fighting disease, a strong attitude can help you ward off misunderstandings. But if you adopt the wrong mindset or make faulty assumptions, you put yourself in a vulnerable position.

Here are the three most dangerous assumptions you can make as a manager in trying to prevent misunderstandings.

1. You assume the other person speaks your language. In today's diverse workplaces, your employees might come from vastly different cultures and backgrounds. They may speak English, but that doesn't mean they understand the subtle shadings of the language or your industry's shorthand.

A supermarket manager once told me he asked a new employee "to face the shelves." Five minutes later, he noticed the employee standing motionless in the middle of the canned soup aisle.

"What are you doing?" he asked the employee.

"I'm doing what you told me," the worker replied.

"I asked you to face the shelves. You're just standing there," the manager said.

It soon dawned on the manager that the employee didn't know that "facing the shelves" meant pulling all the groceries to the front of the shelves, straightening them, and making it easy for shoppers to see the labels.

Define your terms. If you use lingo that's familiar to your longtime colleagues, don't assume new employees know what you mean.

2. You assume people hear everything you say. If you use a word that annoys others, you may lose a chance to make yourself understood. This often happens when managers give feedback to employees. You might say, "You're doing a superb job in processing orders, dealing with customers, and working with our field force. But you're lousy at numbers."

What word will stand out to the employee?

Lousy.

All the praise gets swept away by the mention of just one hurtful or loaded word. The employee will immediately think, "The boss thinks I'm lousy!" not "Wow, I'm doing a superb job in all those areas!"

Replacing "lousy" with a milder description such as "less effective" or "not quite at that excellent level" will send the same message, but without the potential rancor. The employee will appreciate the need to improve without feeling threatened or offended.

3. You assume people want to understand you. Actually, they might have other things on their mind. They may feel under the weather or be preoccupied with a personal problem. The more you talk, the less they listen.

Rather than assume that people are paying attention to you,

Let's Clear That Up...

CAUTION!

You worry about making yourself clear when you're communicating with others at work. So you keep wondering, "Am I being clear?" That's the wrong question. Here's a better one: *"How can I speak in a way that will not be misunderstood?"* Focus less on whether you're speaking clearly and more on making yourself understood.

What's the difference? What's clear to *you* might still be incomprehensible to everyone else. But if you focus on eliminating any chance of being misunderstood, you force yourself to communicate in a manner that's more appropriate for your audience.

---

look for evidence. Are they giving you eye contact? Are they taking notes? Do they signal with their nonverbal cues that they're understanding your points?

If you sense you're not connecting with others, stop and find out why. Ask them if there's anything they want to tell you. Shift from a directive stance to a more attentive, reactive role.

"Testing 1-2-3, ... Testing"

Experienced public speakers check the microphone before they launch into their remarks. Only after members of the audience indicate they can hear fine will the presenter plunge in

Managers who want to avoid misunderstandings should adopt a similar practice in their daily conversations. Rather than dive headlong into a conversation, test the waters first. Make sure everyone's comfortable before proceeding. Here are some examples:

- When you call a colleague or drop by her office, ask, "Is this a good time to discuss the Acme account?"
- When you're about to provide lots of background or details on a complex issue, ask, "Are you ready to go over this now?"
- If you want to delegate a task, say, "I'm going to give you an overview of the assignment and then ask you to confirm I've done a good job explaining it."

A Friendly Game of Telephone

To illustrate the importance of "checking in" with a listener, try this experiment: Gather five employees and invite them to play a game in which the winner has a chance to receive $100. Then position them in a line. Whisper a 20-second message to a player at one end and have that person whisper it to the next person in line, and so forth. When the message reaches the last person in line, compare it with the original. You'll undoubtedly find that the end message barely resembles the original message. Players will often admit that they were so distracted by the prospect of winning $100 that they didn't pay full attention.

Only after you get permission to continue should you advance to the next step. By getting the other person's consent and providing a map of what's about to happen, you'll drastically lower the odds of misunderstanding.

When you test whether it's the right time to communicate, it makes people more attentive. Otherwise, you can wind up sharing important information with a colleague who's preoccupied or simply unable to absorb what you say.

Because most disagreements begin as simple misunderstandings, make extra effort to convey exactly what you want. Also confirm that others are able and willing listen. If you speak clearly and they're ready to soak up your message, you're going to avoid lots of problems.

Learn How to "Groda"

Misunderstandings frequently result when you hear what you want to hear. If you're too eager, excited, or opinionated, you might disregard any comments that don't reinforce what you already think. And if there's any ambiguity in a speaker's remarks, you may twist what you hear so that it fits your preconceived notions.

In my seminars, I introduce managers to a new word: groda. Don't reach for the dictionary; it's not there. I made it up. But once you learn what it means, you won't forget it.

Groda stands for "get rid of dangerous ambiguities." It means removing uncertainties so that you understand precisely what someone's trying to tell you. It also relates to how you speak: pinpoint what you want to say so that there's less room for misinterpretation.

Learning how to groda saves you from daily hassles. You will soon recognize fuzzy statements—made by yourself and others—and take steps to cleanse conversations of vague, cryptic, or downright inscrutable words and phrases.

When I explained the meaning of groda to a purchasing manager, Marisa, she gave me a knowing smile and said, "I wish I knew about that a few months ago." Then she told me about an office-furniture salesperson who dropped by her office to highlight new items for sale.

"When the sales rep was telling me about a new kind of chair, I asked, 'Is it fully adjustable?'" Marisa recalled. "The sales rep didn't really answer yes or no. He just looked pleased and said, 'Check it out for yourself.' Then he showed me a picture of the chair in a sales catalog with a banner across the top that read 'An ergonomic wonder!'"

Marisa interpreted the salesperson's enthusiastic response to her question and the ad in the catalog as a "Yes" (as in "Yes, the chair is fully adjustable."). So she ordered this expensive chair for a vice president at her firm. Minutes after it arrived in his office, he called Marisa and said, "Take it back. I told you I wanted an adjustable chair and this one isn't."

Chagrined, Marisa realized that the salesperson never really answered her question. What's worse, she didn't insist on getting a specific answer. The result: she lost credibility with an influential VP at her company.

Like Marisa, you may have a high tolerance for ambiguity in your everyday conversations. If you ask an employee when an assignment will be completed and he tells you, "I'm working on it," you might take that as a reassuring answer when, in fact, it's not. If you ask for a peer's opinion in a meeting and she says, "I see how you can make that argument," you might walk away

Smart Managing

Insist on an Answer

When you ask a question and the reply does not include the specific information you requested, repeat the question verbatim. Speak in a pleasant tone. Act as if you don't mind having to ask again. If you still don't get a direct answer, ask a third time using the exact same words. This may seem strange at first, but it sends a clear message to others that you really want an answer and you're going to persist-gently but firmly—until you get it.

thinking that person will support your proposal when, in fact, she doesn't.

Ambiguity often leads to problems when you need to criticize or discipline an employee. If you're uncomfortable, you might drop indirect hints and hope the worker reads between the lines. Even worse, you might focus on the positive and barely mention what's negative for fear of discouraging the employee. That's risky. Misunderstandings often occur when managers neglect to speak in a straightforward manner about what's good—and bad—about an individual's performance.

Don't take ambiguity lightly. Unless you're in a negotiation or other delicate situation where you need to strike a noncommittal tone, dig for concrete answers. You may not enjoy what you hear, but at least you'll avoid problems later.

Rushing into Trouble

Surviving as a manager requires a mastery of time. If you're careless or inefficient or you chronically run late, you'll never climb the ladder of success.

Rushing around the office trying to multitask might make you feel productive, but overloading yourself with activity is bound to cause problems. You'll find it hard to listen and concentrate. And that will inevitably lead to misunderstandings.

One example of rushing into trouble can occur when managers schedule meetings but don't allot sufficient time for participants to absorb communication materials such as handouts, fact-filled slides, flow charts, or financial reports. The managers assume that they can distribute materials and employees will

---

Checkpoint Charley

Charley often gave complex instructions to employees by explaining everything at once and handing out a summary sheet. But that didn't work. Employees still struggled to follow the directions. I advised him to explain one step at a time, allow employees to complete it, and then introduce the next step. Ultimately, he created three checkpoints for employees to come to him and say, "That's done, boss. What next?" While it took slightly longer to hold three quick meetings with employees over a few days than to cover everything in one fell swoop, Charley found they caught on much faster and appreciated the chance to ask questions along the way.

---

read them at their leisure and ask questions later. But it rarely works out that way. Unless employees get a chance to analyze and discuss the information in the meeting, they may never truly grasp what you want them to understand.

A harried manager might trigger a related problem by dumping too much information on employees. When the amount of information exceeds a person's capacity to absorb it, the person will typically guess at what information matters most and how to interpret it. When that happens, key parts of your message might get neglected.

Another downside of rushing is it leads to interrupting. If you tend to talk over others and cut them off in mid-sentence, you're inviting problems. You might misunderstand what someone's trying to say and wind up acting on incorrect or incomplete information.

You'll know you're a chronic interrupter if your peers often say, "Let me finish," "I'd appreciate if you'd listen to me," or "Please, this is important. Hear me out." Don't shrug off these comments; treat them as warnings that you're not letting people complete their points.

While managers of all stripes interrupt, research shows that it happens most frequently when men talk with women. Experts who study how gender affects workplace conversation have found that men tend to grow impatient with what they view as women's indirect communication style. As a result, a man

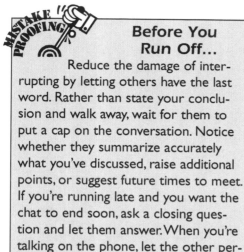

Before You Run Off...

Reduce the damage of interrupting by letting others have the last word. Rather than state your conclusion and walk away, wait for them to put a cap on the conversation. Notice whether they summarize accurately what you've discussed, raise additional points, or suggest future times to meet. If you're running late and you want the chat to end soon, ask a closing question and let them answer. When you're talking on the phone, let the other person be the first to hang up.

might be more prone to trounce on a woman's comments rather than let her finish.

If you habitually interrupt, purse your lips shut. Take notes if that helps you remember what you want to say next. Stoke your curiosity so that you're eager to learn what others think. Derive more satisfaction from listening than talking.

Avoiding Body Language Traps

While describing how he intends to demote an employee, a manager notices the employee nodding vigorously. By the end of the conversation, the manager says, "Well, I'm glad you agree!"

The employee looks confused and wonders, "When did I say that I agree with any of this?"

Beware of nodding if you do not agree with a speaker's remarks. While it's true that an occasional nod can signal understanding and encourage speakers to elaborate, it might also lead them to conclude that you're "on board" with everything they're saying.

Limit your nodding in face-to-face conversations among your colleagues. If a speaker asks, "Am I making sense?" or "Are you with me so far?" that's a good time to nod once. Otherwise, keep still and make sure you're retaining what you hear even if you disagree with it.

An even riskier nonverbal behavior that can trigger misunderstandings involves the silent messages you send with your movements while you're speaking. When you talk with an employee, it's fine to gesture naturally as you maintain eye contact. But if you start to doodle, rifle through papers, or repeatedly glance at the clock, you'll appear nervous or preoccupied. Listeners may doubt what you're saying or grow so distracted that they won't pay full attention.

Keep your hands free when you speak. Put away pens or paper clips so that you don't play with them. If you're unwilling or unable to concentrate, wait until you can free your mind of extraneous worries.

Align yourself with the person with whom you're speaking so that you can communicate at eye level. Sit and stand together so that neither of you towers over the other. When standing, keep your hands resting comfortably at your sides; don't fold your arms across your chest like a drill sergeant.

Strike a receptive pose and you'll reassure others that you're interested in them. You'll also find it easier to decipher what they're saying.

Misunderstandings often start when people don't trust each other or suspect that they're not connecting well. Your confident body language improves the quality of your conversations and helps reinforce your hunger to listen and learn.

Manager's Checklist for Chapter 4

❏ Advance a conversation by asking questions, not making statements.

❏ Wait an extra second after someone stops speaking before you respond.

❏ Paraphrase what you hear by restating a point succinctly. Ask for clarification even when you're fairly sure you got the point the first time.

❏ Give clear instructions to employees. Don't assume they'll pick up on what you left unsaid. And beware of speaking in overly technical jargon or failing to provide proper context for your remarks.

❑ Seek consent from others before you launch into a new topic. Also provide a map of what you're about to cover so the listener can follow along with ease.

❑ Sweep away ambiguities when you speak and listen so that you understand precisely what's being said.

❑ Break complex instructions into digestible chunks to make it simpler for others to understand.

❑ Limit your nodding when you listen. Do not nod if you disagree with a speaker.

Calibrating Your Response

You can either *respond* or *react* to workplace problems. If you *respond*, you can pick the best approach and make sure you convey your points clearly and diplomatically. If you *react*, your mouth can run and you might say things you regret later. What's worse, an impulsive or wildly emotional reaction can make minor problems major.

I'll often ask those managers I admire most, "How do you cope with bad problems at work?" Their answers usually focus on how they stay calm and defuse the stress. Here are some examples:

- "I complete the sentence, 'This could be worse. At least....' That puts things in perspective. I breathe a sigh of relief and then I'm ready to deal with the problem."
- "I need a day to let things sink in. I try not to get too worked up over a problem right when I find out about it."
- "By waiting, I find I'm able to analyze it better. Of course, I can't do this if it's a true crisis that requires immediate action."

- "I like to walk it off. When I try too quickly to address a problem, I act rashly. I find the first 15-minute block of time I can spare and do a speed walk for a few blocks. I return to the office refreshed and able to think more clearly."

These managers wisely detach themselves from the problem so that they can evaluate it with a clear mind. They don't lose their temper or curse their bad luck (or at least they don't admit to it!). Instead, they seek some form of emotional control. Then they calibrate their response and get to work.

Learn from their example. *Respond* rather than *react* to problems. Consider adopting one of the above techniques to cope with a sudden, serious problem. Sweep away excess stress so that you can assess the situation accurately and act decisively.

Flipping the Emotional Light Switch

Perhaps you're familiar with research indicating that women exhibit emotion more readily than men and that men tend to react with more visible anger and agitation when facing problems. Don't take that as a general rule.

Both men and women can snap at an underling for making a costly error. Both can rant or go into a tizzy. Both can take out their frustration by throwing tantrums. The real issue is how *all* of us harness our emotions so that we solve problems most effectively.

Reducing the negative effects of problems starts with emotional control. Maintaining your composure when mishaps arise gives you an instant advantage. Here's what you gain by keeping cool:

- **You instill confidence.** Your colleagues will follow your lead if you stay composed. They will limit their own displays of panic or anger if you model the kind of level-headed clarity you seek.

- **You conserve energy.** By pausing, taking a deep breath, and striving to address a difficult problem, you don't let the histrionics of overreacting sap your energy. You also save time and test solutions faster.
- **You think more clearly.** It's easier to solve problems when your mind is free of clutter. Swirling anxiety or simmering fury can prevent you from thinking at your best.

Enroll in an anger-management workshop and one of the first things you'll learn is to recognize the feelings that can lead you to blow your stack. If you instinctively react to problems by pounding a fist on your desk or cursing your bad luck to anyone within earshot, then you need to back up and identify what sets you off and what alternate strategies you can adopt.

Imagine a light switch in your head. When you're informed of a problem at work, you can flip the switch and light up the room with your anger and irritation. Or you can leave the switch in the "off" setting and methodically decide what to do next. That's the key to responding—not reacting—to setbacks.

Keeping a leash on your emotions doesn't mean you must act like a robot. It's often appropriate or at least understandable to respond to big problems

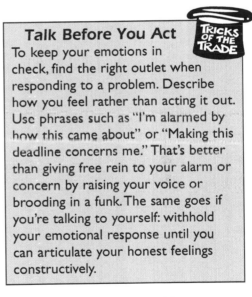

Talk Before You Act

To keep your emotions in check, find the right outlet when responding to a problem. Describe how you feel rather than acting it out. Use phrases such as "I'm alarmed by how this came about" or "Making this deadline concerns me." That's better than giving free rein to your alarm or concern by raising your voice or brooding in a funk. The same goes if you're talking to yourself: withhold your emotional response until you can articulate your honest feelings constructively.

with the "three A's:" anger, annoyance, and anxiety. Trying to suppress such feelings entirely rarely works.

The danger lies in succumbing to destructive emotions. Indulging in bouts of stewing rage or resentment can alienate allies who could otherwise help you fix what's broken. What's worse, letting slip just one hostile comment can plunge your

When Firing Away Backfires

A former engineer with NTL, a big cable company, recalled in a *New York Times* interview an unpleasant meeting with his boss. "All [my boss] wanted to talk about was how high the shares were trading and how great NTL was," he said. But when he raised concerns about the high employee turnover in the engineering department, his boss snapped, "If you don't like it, we can hire someone else" (*The New York Times*, February 7, 2002, p. W1). That's precisely the wrong way for a manager to treat an employee who raises a problem in good faith.

employees into the depths of despair and prolong whatever problem you're facing.

Taking Stock: The Need for Perspective

If you're upset at yourself, a few minutes of venting should help. But controlling your anger gets harder when a coworker ticks you off. You may wind up focusing your anger on the person (or group) whom you perceive as the cause of the problem.

Your rational side tells you that exploding at someone—even someone who deserves a good tongue-lashing—won't resolve anything. In fact, you know deep down it'll probably make a bad situation worse. But when your irrational side takes over, the sparks can fly.

Before you blow up at others, consider the context. Does the issue at hand really merit such a strong reaction? Has your colleague committed a major offense or done irreparable harm? Will coming down hard help you reach a solution faster?

Unless you can honestly answer "Yes" to these questions— and that's extremely improbable—then you're better off maintaining perspective. Ask yourself, "What would happen if I just took it in stride?" You may realize the smartest problem-solving strategy is to stay in control and weigh your options in a calm, reasonable frame of mind.

When problems erupt, the emotions you experience aren't random. There's a reason that you feel betrayed, scared, or agitated. Try to search for the triggers that cause your anger or upset.

Say you're steaming because an employee assured you he'd deliver an important report to you by 10:00 a.m. today. Now it's noon and you're still waiting. You're already rehearsing some choice words you're going to "share" with the employee later.

A wiser approach is to step back and reflect on your anger. Are you furious because the employee didn't do his job? Or is there another, possibly deeper trigger?

> **Another Set of Ears**
>
> **Smart Managing**
>
> Before you give in to your worst emotions, get a second opinion from a dispassionate source. Ask a trusted friend for his or her views on the situation. Call or meet face-to-face with this person. (Don't do it by e-mail.) Explain the problem and why you're so peeved about it. Then ask for advice. You may find that your friend offers a fresh interpretation of the event and provides perspective on what happened, why it happened, and what to do next.

Plumbing your emotions to discover what's driving them can prove revealing. You may realize that your anger is triggered by the embarrassment you'll face when your boss learns that you can't get your employees to meet simple deadlines. Or your anger may flow from your disgust at your apparent inability to delegate properly. You may even find that you're overreacting because of unrelated personal or professional pressures that are just too raw or intense to confront head on.

By assessing the underlying source of your discord, you gain self-awareness that can help you redirect your anger toward productive problem solving. Once you detect the subtle triggers that contribute to your emotional flare-ups, you can keep your perspective and respond with a cool head.

Getting Past Grudges

When Michael called me, he could barely stand being in the same room with Joe, his partner on a project team. He wanted advice on how to get along with Joe, "a former friend" who now grated on him.

It turns out Michael held a grudge against Joe from a few

weeks earlier. That's when Joe accepted a lunch invitation from the company president without telling Michael, much less asking the president if Michael could come along.

While the two partners weren't openly feuding, Michael told me he couldn't concentrate on his work anymore. "I just don't trust Joe, but I have to work closely with him day in and day out," he said. "It's eating away at me."

Grudges can take on a life all their own. Many managers who butt heads with associates or suffer perceived slights tend to cling to their irritation like a life raft. It's as if they just don't want to let go, put aside their differences, and work productively with others.

If you harbor resentment toward a peer, here's the hard truth: You need to talk it out with the person *now*. Don't procrastinate. Don't assume time will heal all wounds. Don't avoid the individual and hope he or she quits. Those passive measures will only exacerbate your problem.

Use this five-step process to express your grievance and salvage your working relationship:

1. **Hash it out.** Meet with the other person and discuss your grudge. Explain that your intent isn't to stir up trouble, but to work together on resolving a problem with the relationship. Describe in fair, non-accusatory terms why you're upset and what happened to make you feel that way.

2. **Cite examples.** Be ready to give dates, times, and instances that support your concerns. Don't just say, "I'm riled by how you operate behind my back." Prepare concrete examples, such as last Thursday's meeting where you felt ostracized or the fact you weren't invited to lunch with the president a week ago.

3. **Stop and listen.** Give the other person a chance to speak. Ask questions such as "What do you think?" or "Does this make sense?" and then keep quiet. As you listen, focus on whether your feelings stem from the initial problem or if new issues muddy the picture. Above all, don't jump

from one grievance to another. Limit your discussion to one problem at a time and give the other person ample time to respond.

4. **Show interest and follow up on what you hear.** Ask more questions. Demonstrate eagerness to learn from the other person. Use this step to gather the information you need to work through your grievance.

5. **Agree on a solution.** Finalize what must happen to resolve the problem. Work together to address mutual concerns. Ideally, both of you should take some responsibility and commit to a positive action plan.

If you're like most people I advise, you probably dread the idea of discussing your grudge with the person you resent. Perhaps you've reached a point where you simply prefer to avoid the person or people who upset you. That's certainly one way to cope, but it's not a long-term solution.

Sweep away lingering bitterness. You'll respond more fairly and favorably to colleagues if you can see them for who they really are. Maybe they made mistakes and misbehaved. Maybe they showed poor judgment or betrayed your trust. But unless you level with them about your concerns and grievances, you create an environment that's ripe for more problems

The Power of Negative Thinking

Norman Vincent Peale, a pioneer of self-help, wrote the classic book *The Power of Positive Thinking* in 1952. Since then, hundreds of authors have carried the positive-thinking torch to new highs.

Maybe there's another side to the story.

When mishaps occur, you may calibrate your response based on how well you can reframe a problem as an opportunity. You may also try to "see the silver lining," treat it as a "blessing in disguise," or "turn lemons into lemonade." That's all well and good—but there's a catch.

Recent research indicates our faith in positive thinking may

Key Term **Defensive pessimism** A deliberate, structured focus on emergency planning and negative contingencies. It involves three steps:
- Approach the problem with lowered expectations (i.e., assuming it'll go badly).
- Identify in detail all the specific ways things can go wrong.
- Plan ways to avert each disastrous outcome.

be overblown. Julie K. Norem, a psychologist at Wellesley College and author of *The Positive Power of Negative Thinking* (New York: Basic Books, 2001), believes that adopting a sunny, upbeat frame of mind isn't necessarily the best problem-solving approach. In fact, she argues that too much positive thinking can actually *induce* anxiety rather than *alleviate* it.

Norem recommends responding to challenges or adversity by considering negative outcomes. As contrary as it sounds, you can sometimes heighten your peace of mind by engaging in alarmist or worst-case thinking. It just takes a mastery of "defensive pessimism."

Do you want to test the benefits of defensive pessimism? Think of a problem you face or a task on your to-do list that you dread. Now follow these three steps:

1. **Assume the worst.** Ratchet down your expectations. For example, if you're struggling to convince a group of employees to address their faltering performance, don't think, "Oh, if I just keep plugging away and making my case, they'll shape up." Replace that with doomsday thoughts such as "It's clear to me that these employees are past the point of no return. They're lost causes. They're going to bring this whole company down with them."

2. **Pick at the scab.** Think about all the ensuing problems you'll face as a result of your lowered expectations. Imagine how your problems can compound or spread like a virus. If your employees are performing poorly, you may think, "They'll cost us our biggest account. They'll drive

Will Negative Thinking Work for You?

Use this checklist to determine if you're a good candidate for experimenting with negative thinking as a problem-solving strategy:

- ❏ When I learn of a problem, I worry about it right away.
- ❏ I expect minor problems to multiply into major ones.
- ❏ When one thing goes wrong, I wait for something else to go wrong.
- ❏ When someone assures me, "It'll be fine" or "Don't worry," I never believe it.
- ❏ I've been burned before for assuming a problem would take care of itself.

If you checked one or more of these statements, give defensive pessimism a try. To learn more, read *The Positive Power of Negative Thinking*.

away new business. They'll contaminate new hires with their rotten attitude. They'll file a lawsuit against us."

3. **Stop the bleeding.** Take each dark, woeful scenario you dreamed up and consider how to prevent it. Draft detailed plans and strategies that defuse risks and extinguish fires before they rage out of control.

Embracing defensive pessimism can empower you to combat problems in a can do, proactive manner. Norem suggests that this counterintuitive approach works especially well for managers who're naturally anxious. The ability to psyche themselves *down*—not *up*—enables them to anticipate and disarm each potential catastrophe before it engulfs them.

This gloom-and-doom response to problems isn't for everyone. If you're a diehard optimist, there's no reason to abandon your positive attitude. But if you identify more readily with darkness than light, it's worth a try.

Following de Gaulle's Rules

The French statesman Charles de Gaulle explained his success in resisting the German occupation in World War II by citing three rules. He was committed to staying "in with the outs," exploiting the inevitable, and avoiding getting stuck between a dog and a lamppost. He conquered far more problems than most managers ever will by using these rules to guide his response.

Follow de Gaulle's lead. Use his three-prong strategy for working your way through problems.

Stay "In with the Outs"

Maintain a vast network of allies both inside and outside your organization. Your web of supporters will buffer you from the worst damage when problems arise. For instance, woo out-of-favor executives or "malcontents" whom other managers dismiss. They can feed you vital information and provide insights that you might not get from anyone else.

A senior vice president at a financial services company once told me jokingly that the secret to his career success was his talent for "making friends with the lepers." He meant that by befriending the back-office supervisors and unheralded grunts who produced the bulk of the work, he cultivated a base of support that he drew upon whenever he confronted a problem.

When adversity strikes, you may need to seek help from workers at all levels. If you're already on good terms with a diverse mix of peers, employees, and higher-ups, you'll find it much easier to mobilize them to pull together to clean up a mess.

To stay in with the outs, you'll need to rise above petty animosities and bridge cultural gaps. Individuals branded as troublemakers or rabble-rousers by the top brass are usually ostracized by fast-track managers. Keep an open mind about these folks. Invite them to lunch, learn what motivates them, and show interest in their work and their aspirations. Even if they don't fall within your direct chain of command, it's still wise to forge ties so that they're on your side when you need them.

Exploit the Inevitable

Managers who survive organizational turmoil and professional setbacks conserve their energy. They respond to problems that they can solve and limit their involvement in the ones they cannot control. They don't drop everything and storm around in a huff when their boss quits or a computer glitch forces them to enter data manually. They simply accept the inevitable and move on.

Say your organization faces impending layoffs. The president has hinted strongly that downsizing has to occur soon, so you have a choice: You can either go about your business as if nothing's amiss or plan to tackle the problem and devise potential solutions. Burying your head in the sand might help you cope in the short term, but you'll suffer later when the inevitable storm hits as pink slips get passed out.

A smart manager thinks ahead. What happens when the CEO announces layoffs? How will things change? What's at stake?

Exploiting the inevitable might lead you to create an informal resource center to encourage at-risk employees to get a head start on career planning. For example, you can arrange for workers to take personality tests or career aptitude exams that give them a better sense of directions to pursue. Or you can offer to pay for employees who enroll in night classes to expand their skills or earn a professional designation.

These steps will not only prepare your employees more effectively if they're laid off. It also demonstrates your proactive response to a brewing problem—a sure sign that you're a top manager who's thinking one step ahead.

Avoid Standing Between a Dog and a Lamppost

When you get stuck in the wrong place at the wrong time, problems become even more annoying and painful to tackle. Rather than respond in a calm, focused manner, you may berate yourself for allowing this to happen. You may engage in bouts of recrimination ("Why didn't I...?" "What's wrong with me?" "What was I thinking?") that will only add to your anger. And when you're spent and exhausted, you'll still face the same problem but with less energy to fight it.

Take preventive steps to avoid problems. Whenever possible, don't put yourself in a vulnerable position. This way, when you hit snags you can respond forcefully without kicking yourself at the same time.

Discipline That Sinks In

One of the hardest aspects of managing employees is responding appropriately when they misbehave. Whether it's carelessness, meanness, or negligence, you can't let their antics go unnoticed or you invite more of the same. You want to lay down the law. But you fear coming down too hard and turning them into whimpering or bitter foes.

There's no single right way to discipline employees. Your tone and word choice will depend on the personality of the individual. An aggressive, hard-edged person might treat your message more seriously if you deliver it in a stern, no-nonsense staccato ("You have to shape up, get it right the first time, stop goofing off, stop blaming others, and learn to enjoy it here"), while a person who's more sensitive or eager to please might prefer if you take a less strident tone ("I realize you're trying hard. Let me suggest some ways you can see better results").

Discipline works best when it comes as no surprise to employees. They should already know what rules apply to them, what standards they must meet, and when they cross a

---

⚠ CAUTION!

Loosen Your Grip

A frequent mistake managers make when disciplining is they lecture too much. If you sound like a teacher scolding a pupil, you're going too far. Humanize your message by inserting some "disclosure" about how *you* feel or how *you* see the situation. Examples:

- "I'm not sure how to make you aware of this."
- "I'm torn in terms of whether to take disciplinary action against you."
- "I'm left with only a few options, and none of them are all that pleasant."

Then ask the employee to chime in. That grants him or her at least some control, even if just temporarily. But that small gesture can make a big difference in making the employee more receptive to what you're about to say.

line that you deem unacceptable. Workers should never be shocked when you alert them of their misdeeds, except on those occasions when you point out something they had no way of knowing was wrong.

Some managers confess to me that they're uncomfortable having to discipline certain employees or even intimidated by them. As a result, they pretend not to notice poor performance or outlandish behavior in the hope it'll go away on its own.

That rarely happens.

If you dread the prospect of disciplining someone, role-play with a colleague. Rehearse what you'll say and do and how you'll respond to the employee's likely questions and objections. Then take the plunge. Realize that each time you have these difficult conversations with employees, you practice your communication skills and become a better manager. Heed the wisdom of Benjamin Franklin, who advised a friend that it was fine to read a book about how to swim, but there was no substitute for jumping in the water and testing whether you've really learned what you need to learn.

Manager's Checklist for Chapter 5

❏ *Respond* rather than *react* to problems. Map out a strategy for addressing them so that you're not acting on impulse.

❏ Wait to react emotionally to a problem until you state your honest feelings constructively. This alone can help you calm down.

❏ Before you lose your temper, consider the context. Determine if the problem truly merits such a strong reaction.

❏ If you hold a grudge against someone, don't let it fester. Talk it out with the person and honestly express your concerns.

❏ Respond to tough, dreaded problems by conjuring up worst-case scenarios. Then plan for them and take proactive steps to address them.

Solving the Seven Biggest On-the-Job Conflicts

*C*heck *your emotions at the door.* That's the unwritten rule governing most workplace behavior. You're supposed to take everything in stride, smile and frown on cue, and never lose control. In reality, however, most people who try to deaden their emotions find it impossible to maintain their equanimity 100% of the time. It's just not natural.

Many employees prefer to work with colleagues who stay on an even keel and do not display emotional highs and lows on the job. According to research by Michael Kramer and Jon Hess, communication professors at the University of Missouri-Columbia, workers do not want their colleagues to express *any* type of strong emotion—negative or positive.

The researchers surveyed employees from a range of occupations and asked them to describe situations where emotions were managed "appropriately" or "inappropriately." They found that the only "appropriate" way for employees to manage negative feelings at work was to mask them. The respondents viewed the ability to hide adverse emotions as a sign of professionalism.

The researchers also found that employees prefer coworkers who bury their positive emotions by not showing too much pleasure with promotions or raises. Why? They feared that fist-pumping antics by an ambitious career climber could sow resentment in others who miss out. Their findings point to a potentially flammable situation in many workplaces: unless employees suppress their feelings and adopt a middle-of-the-road demeanor at all times, their flashes of emotion can alienate and disturb their peers.

What Kramer and Hess call "emotion management"—the ability to control and modulate feelings—is not taught at work. Individuals become socialized by watching how others act. That's their guide to determine what's acceptable and unacceptable behavior.

In practice, however, suppressing strong feelings isn't a particularly realistic or even healthy goal when you're emotionally invested in your job and the people around you. What's more, on-the-job conflicts arise constantly. Emotional reactions are unavoidable.

A more practical strategy involves anticipating and responding effectively to common situations that trigger extreme emotions. If you're aware that a certain set of circumstances can lead you to feel irate or hurt, for example, you can gird yourself for the experience and monitor your emotional state.

With that in mind, let's examine the best way to respond to seven of the most prevalent conflicts that can erupt at work.

1. "There's Not Enough Time!"

In many workplaces, every day is a race against time. It's like a game show with a clock that never stops winding down. But instead of valuable prizes for the winner, at best you get to survive and advance to the next round with the same timer ticking away.

Conflicts that revolve around lack of time often lead managers to cut corners and make hasty decisions without all the information they'd ideally like at their fingertips. They may figure, "I'm under the gun here, so I can't afford to think this through."

When you're rushing to extinguish fires, pressure provides a great excuse for sloppy work or hurried decisions. Yet a time crunch does not free you from responsibility for your actions. You still need to weigh decisions with care and collect your thoughts before you make commitments.

If you're racing to complete work under tight time constraints and tempers start to flare, pause, take a deep breath, and look ahead 24 hours. Analyze how you'll spend each of those hours. Identify the lowest-priority task you face during that time frame and postpone it. That will give you an extra pocket of time as a cushion to focus on what matters most.

Say it's 10:00 a.m. and you learn your top client has threatened to cancel all orders unless certain mistakes get corrected immediately. You know this problem requires your full attention. You check your daily planner and see that you have two job candidates scheduled later today to come in for second interviews. You're tempted to squeeze in the interviews because you hate to delay the hiring process, but you wisely have an assistant call to reschedule them. This gives you the buffer you need to work productively without undue rushing.

Smart Managing

Reposition Your Mental Clock

Your productivity can falter if you're so preoccupied with impending deadlines that you struggle to concentrate on the work at hand. To clear your mind and relieve at least some of the pressure, imagine you're working in 15-minute blocks. Set mini-goals that you want to attain within each quarter hour. Complete the sentence, "In the next 15 minutes, I will accomplish...." Then rivet your attention solely on finishing your immediate to-do task. Continue setting mini-goals throughout the day and you'll beat the clock while saving yourself from excess anxiety.

---

2. "This Is Spiraling out of Control!"

If you believe in Murphy's Law, then you expect that if anything can go wrong, it will. And if you're prone to believe that one mishap will mushroom into another ... and then another, you probably often wind up thinking, "This situation's out of control."

Labeling a problem "out of control" can prove liberating to someone who feels mired in crises. Once it's deemed uncontrollable, you can give up trying to do anything positive to solve it. You simply shrug, try to forget about it, and wait for the next shoe to drop.

But savvy managers know a problem that's spiraling out of control can still be treated or at least mitigated to some extent. For instance, you can anticipate outcomes and plan for them. And by enlisting others to help, you can develop ways to track the problem's ripple effects so that you're ready to contain the damage.

The next time you face a seemingly insurmountable problem, don't fret about how it's growing or how you're never going to rein in what looks like a runaway crisis. These thoughts will only make you panic or feel helpless.

It's better to detach yourself and take an Olympian view of the situation. Pretend you're narrating the situation in the third person or telling a bedtime story to a child. Describe each aspect of the problem as a disengaged observer. You might replace "This just keeps getting worse!" with "After the first error was discovered in the brochure, another typo soon came to our attention." This may sound silly at first, but it's actually a great way to process negative news without taking it too hard.

The simple act of describing a problem in a factual, here's-

Here's My Problem ...

When an insurance agent told me about a problem that just kept getting worse, she started off by saying, "It was so terrible. It was like a nightmare. Everything fell apart." I stopped her and told her to narrate what happened rather than editorialize. She took a breath and said, "The insurer I worked with increased its premiums 40% while scaling back its coverage. I convinced my clients to renew their policies anyway. They were upset, but they trusted me. Then the insurer pulled out of our state and stopped writing policies entirely. My clients were really worried now. Finally, the state insurance department announced they were investigating the insurer for unfair claim practices." Let the facts speak for themselves.

what-happened-next manner serves as a springboard to solving it. Try to talk like *Star Trek*'s Dr. Spock so that you can grasp the full dimension or complexity of what's going on without panicking.

From that point, you can assess what to do next without feeling as if you're sinking in quicksand. The problem may very well be spiraling out of control, but repeatedly saying that won't make it any more manageable.

3. "I Don't Trust You!"

During the presidency of Ronald Reagan, "trust but verify" served as a baseline belief that shaped negotiations between Americans and Russians. The subtext was *we want to trust you, and we're willing to trust you, but we're not going to trust you blindly.*

That same philosophy can help you manage work-related situations in which trust has broken down. By adopting trust-building measures and taking steps to prove your good faith along the way, you can ratchet down suspicions and divisiveness among your staff.

Left unchecked, lack of trust can turn petty squabbles into major conflicts. Problems worsen when warring parties view each other with doubt and disdain. What often saves minor run-ins among employees from escalating into head-on collisions is

TRICKS OF THE TRADE

Let's Make a List

To cultivate trust between two employees, meet with them privately. Give them a sheet of paper with two columns headed "Reasons to Trust" and "Reasons Not to Trust." Have them list reasons to trust each other and reasons not to. Assure them that the purpose of this exercise is to help you—and them—get a better handle on the problem. Promise confidentiality. If they list plenty of reasons in the "not to trust" column but have trouble coming up with entries for the other column, help them seek balance. Remind them of trustworthy actions each has taken and cite examples of successful projects they've worked on together.

the ability of the manager to coax combatants to acknowledge the underlying trust they've built up.

A sure-fire way to foster trust is to create a trust-but-verify tracking system. That way, even if you cannot induce skeptics to lower their guard at first, you can incrementally convince each of them that they stand by their word. Take the following four steps.

1. Document the rift. Work with the individuals to prepare a joint statement in writing that summarizes the problem and the need for trust.

Example: "We use the honor system when making withdrawals from the petty-cash fund for office expenses and team outings. But this has led to disagreement over who's spending the money and whether it's being spent appropriately."

2. Draft an agreement. Stipulate a solution to the problem. You can't impose trust, but you can clarify the intentions of both parties and outline what they can do to work together in a productive, trust-building fashion.

Example: "The solution is to keep a log of petty-cash withdrawals that includes the date and purpose of each expenditure."

3. Devise a monitoring system and timetable for implementation. Decide how everyone can measure the results. Remove any doubt about who's doing what, how it's tabulated, and your expectations for gradual trust building.

Example: "You will each have access to the log at any time. If anyone has any questions or concerns about the accuracy of the log, please see me. We will use the log for three months and assess the results. At that time, we agree to consider whether to terminate the log and return to the honor system."

4. Address "what if" concerns. Specify the consequences if either party does not abide by the agreement. It's often effective to bind the employees together by indicating that both will face penalties if either of them breaches the trust.

Example: "If the steps above are not followed, further action can be taken, including a range of disciplinary measures. Both of you will share in the consequences equally, regardless of alleged fault."

4. "You Broke Your Promise!"

Trust rests on commitments that people make to each other, both implied and explicit. If these commitments are abandoned or broken without prior notice and mutual consent, problems tend to worsen. Despite your best efforts, your unit can crumble as employees treat each other as untrustworthy and devious foes.

Broken promises often arise from simple misunderstandings, rather than malice or calculated dissembling. If James says he'll deliver certain items to Randy by Friday but fails to do so, he may later claim he only promised he would do everything he could to order the items and arrange for delivery on a timely basis. In any case, Randy no longer believes James.

It's typical blame shifting. The long-term result is they grow more suspicious of each other and their ill will infects the entire office. If you're managing James and Randy, you need to help them appreciate each other's frame of reference.

> **Key Term**
> **Blame shifting** The act of ducking responsibility after making a promise and redirecting onto some abstract entity when that promise isn't met. This can take the form of *scapegoating*, where the guilty party diverts attention from himself or herself by accusing an innocent bystander of wrongdoing.

Suggest to Randy that James didn't deliberately lie; instead, he underestimated his ability to fulfill his commitment. That doesn't free James of blame, of course, but it does capture the situation more accurately.

At the same time, you'll want to help James consider Randy's point of view. You might say to James, "You know, Randy now questions any promise you make. He feels you made him look bad by not delivering those items. The way he sees it, he accepted your promise at face value, assured others he'd get the material as you said, and wound up with egg on his face. But he's not out to get you now, and you have a golden opportunity to convince him you're trustworthy by being more clear and then coming through next time."

By holding one-on-one discussions with each employee, you can pry their minds open to work together again amicably. Once they start to make new promises to each other and follow through on them, they can overcome their differences.

Whenever coworkers square off over a broken promise, hold them accountable for their past and present actions. Don't let them shift the focus away from themselves unless or until they admit their role and provide full disclosure of what they said and did that contributed to the problem.

5. "I'll Win This Battle!"

If you've read this far, you've learned at least one fundamental lesson of managing problems: words matter. The language you use to characterize conflict will influence how you feel about it. Speak in neutral or positive terms and you'll keep your negative emotions at bay.

Easy to say, tough to do.

Some managers equate conflicts with war. They favor military metaphors that carry an "us vs. them" confrontational tone. Adopting this outlook exacerbates conflict because it objectifies others as "the enemy" and frames problems as do-or-die "battles" in which the only solution is total victory.

Framing workplace conflicts as battles hurts your cause. You'll wind up taking an adversarial stance rather than seeking compromise. You may hunker down, brace for skirmishes, and expect others to act badly or resist you every step of the way.

You'll know you're in trouble if you weave warlike imagery into your speaking. Examples:

- "I'm shooting down your proposal."
- "If we firebomb them, that'll work."
- "You hit me and I'll pound you with everything I've got."

Hitting a Wall

Stan protested when I told him to lighten up on the war talk. As a middle manager frustrated with his inability to earn promotions, he blamed jealous, conniving peers at his firm. Instead of trying to understand their needs, he adopted a stubborn, must-win attitude that led to constant run-ins with his colleagues. At one point, Stan defended his behavior by quoting Ferdinand Foch, the French general at the Battle of the Marne in 1914, "Victory will come to the side that outlasts the other." Stan simply refused to budge—and he's now unemployed.

There's nothing wrong with taking an aggressive position toward external competitors, especially if the message from your organization's senior executives is to trounce a rival company. But if you perceive your coworkers as foes whom you must fight, then even if you "win" you'll spread distrust and discord among your team.

Your conflicts will intensify when you treat bosses or coworkers as opponents. Your eagerness to do battle will prevent you from considering constructive, problem-solving possibilities. Worst of all, you may use your hostility as an excuse to hurt others the way you feel they've hurt you. That strategy almost guarantees your work life will become more miserable than ever.

The next time you're tempted to speak—or think—in warlike metaphors, reframe the situation in less militaristic terms. Banish words such as "battle," "war," and "bomb" from your vocabulary when you're referring to your relations with coworkers. Instead, talk about how you'll "listen," "learn," and "team up." Examples:

- Replace "I've got a real battle going on with the underwriters" with "I'm going to learn what the underwriters need."
- Replace "I'll drop a bomb on my boss that he'll never forget" with "I'll listen and then present an airtight case to my boss."
- Replace "This is a war I can win with those bean counters" with "Teaming up with the accountants should help us both."

6. "How Dare You Say That?!"

Taking offense at what someone says—and making a fuss about it—rarely works to your advantage. Unless a coworker utters a flagrantly racist, sexist, obscene, or otherwise unacceptable comment (in which case you feel compelled to object), it's usually best either to ignore inappropriate comments or dig for more information.

Many managers find it especially hard to listen to criticism. They might tense up whenever a boss, peer, or employee says, "You're not very good at..." or "One thing you need to work on is...."

Limit your outbursts of indignation. Rather than exclaim, "How dare you?!" keep quiet until you collect your thoughts and absorb the speaker's full message. Realize that waiting to state your disapproval can work better than instinctively protesting something the moment you hear it.

Welcome constructive criticism even if it hurts. Invite the speaker to expand by asking earnest, curious follow-up questions. Examples:

- "When does this tend to happen? Have you noticed any patterns?"
- "What's an example of this?"
- "Do you think it's getting worse lately?"
- "How long have you thought this?"
- "What led you to tell me this now?"

Through these questions, asked with genuine interest, you can spark a healthy dialogue that clarifies the problem and shifts smoothly to proposed solutions.

Even if you think the speaker could've been more diplomatic in criticizing you, that's still no reason to react with outrage. Some people lack tact. Anyone who's going to survive the potholes of management must develop a thick skin and endure rough remarks.

Befriend your critics. The more they like you, the less incentive they'll have to share their criticism about you with others.

My Invisible Twin

TRICKS OF THE TRADE When you hear stinging criticism, pretend it's directed at a close friend. You want to help your "friend," so you listen openly, probe to learn more, and develop strategies to address the speaker's concerns. Confirm that you understand the gist of the criticism by frequently paraphrasing. Detach yourself from the discussion and you'll find it easier to gather information and process it in a fair-minded manner. Your "friend" will benefit greatly from your efforts!

Share ideas on how you can improve and hash out an action plan to show that you take to heart what they say.

If you disagree with the criticism, say so without rancor. Cite facts that support your view rather than lapse into defensiveness.

Consider how Susan, a merchandising manager, handled a situation when her boss lambasted her hard work in creating a new marketing campaign and declared it a "big disappointment." Susan didn't flinch, back down, or stew in anger. Instead, she said in a calm and slightly surprised tone, "I thought we generated five new clients thanks to my marketing campaign." At first, her boss disagreed and they debated the results. But with each fact Susan added, she undercut her boss's position even more and eventually resolved the issue to her advantage.

"Go into data-gathering mode when you're tempted to get angry at someone," suggests Frank McNair, a North Carolina-based management consultant. "When in doubt, probe. Otherwise, your anger might inflame the conflict without accomplishing anything. You won't look good. You won't save time. And it won't do much good to act all outraged if it doesn't change anyone's mind."

7. "I Know Better than You!"

Some of the worst conflicts erupt over who's right and who's wrong. All the listening, patience, and open-mindedness in the world won't help if you're certain you know what's best for someone but your words fall upon deaf ears.

Resolving right-wrong disputes begins only after you accept a fundamental premise: before working toward a mutually satisfying solution, you must first demonstrate that you understand the other person's views. If you've got a problem with an employee, give a fair, accurate description of the issue from the employee's perspective before you offer your opinion.

The Limits of Talking

If your goal is to get employees to accept that you're right, stop talking and start prompting them to prove it to themselves. Research shows that people retain 10% of what they read, 20% of what they hear, 30% of what they see, 50% of what they see and hear, 70% of what they say, and 90% of what they say and apply. So mitigate problems by encouraging employees to state the benefits of what you suggest and apply those benefits to produce the results they want.

Most people don't like being proved wrong. If you're too strident in asserting your position, you might establish your rightness but jeopardize your ability to forge a productive working relationship.

Rookie managers can discover this lesson the hard way. They may lay down the law and enforce strict new rules, only to find that resentful employees quietly sabotage them. The problem soon intensifies as the managers issue more sweeping edicts or more restrictive rules. Before too long, a mutiny erupts.

Even if you know you're right and you're unwilling to waver, beware of imposing your knowledge so strongly that you squash others' views. This can lead to "malicious compliance"—your employees heed your directives on the surface while growing disillusioned working for you. Your success as manager ultimately depends not just on whether employees comply, but whether they believe *you're* learning from *them* and respecting their contribution.

Manager's Checklist for Chapter 6

❏ If you're squeezed for time, work in 15-minute blocks. Set mini-goals to cap off each quarter hour.

❏ Describe a problem in a factual, detached manner so that you can solve it with a clear head. Beware of overdramatizing it.

❏ Lead employees to take trust-building measures. Have them document the source of their distrust and the steps they're willing to take to work together.

❏ When employees break their promises to you or each other, it may be because of a misunderstanding. Rather than brand anybody a liar, discuss what happened without pointing fingers.

❏ Speak in positive terms to mitigate conflicts. Avoid war metaphors. Replace words such as "battle" and "bomb" with "listen" and "team up."

❏ Limit outbursts of indignation. Rather than say "How dare you?!" keep quiet and withhold judgment until you're sure you understand the speaker's entire message in context.

❏ Respond to criticism by probing to learn more. Don't defend yourself.

❏ To convince others that you're right, get them to summarize your point and apply it so that they can see for themselves.

Thinking Like a Scientist

Samantha couldn't believe her staff's poor attitude or declining performance. She'd say to me, "If only I had done things differently" or "I should've never let them get away with that." Her distress would soon devolve into mini-tirades where she'd lash out at herself, her bosses, her employees, even her parents!

After a few sessions with her, I knew she needed more than to vent. So I told her, "Make your emotions work *for* you, not *against* you." I suggested that she transform her agitation into energy—intellectual fuel she could use to think of creative solutions.

When you're facing a problem, weighing what action to take to solve it empowers you to charge ahead. But if you dwell on your regrets, anger, or irritation, you won't get very far. As I like to tell managers who are stymied by problems, "How you *feel* matters, but what you *do* matters much more."

Many managers react to problems on an impulsive, emotional level. When they discover a mishap, they may think:

"That was so stupid of me!"
"I'm so fed up with these things happening!"
"This will make me look bad!"

Sadly, it doesn't stop there. When you mentally kick yourself and think, "That was so stupid of me!" it's often followed by a litany of other self-berating thoughts such as "I'm a goner in this job" or "I wonder how else I've screwed up." It's like eating potato chips: one bad thought isn't enough so you get hooked on them. Within minutes, you're stuck in a downhill spiral of gloom-and-doom hopelessness and mounting agitation.

While it's unrealistic to remove all emotion from solving problems, you can work your way out of a mess more quickly by thinking dispassionately about what to do. Complaining, chastising, and blaming yourself—or others—wastes time and usually compounds whatever problem you're already up against.

Consider how trained scientists respond to setbacks. They don't stomp their feet when experiments fail or let their tempers interfere with their ability to assess problems appropriately. Instead, they identify what caused the unwanted result and what actions to take to achieve a better outcome the next time.

Scientists thrive on measurable data. They devote great care to tracking data, tabulating it, and confirming its accuracy. When things go wrong, they review the information they've collected and look for answers buried in the data.

Tricks of the Trade — First Reactions

When you discover a problem, notice the first thought that pops into mind. If you think, "What next?" or "What do I know and what do I need to find out to solve it?" you're on the right track. But if you fret, panic, or instinctively think about who's to blame, you're already setting yourself up for even more disappointment and frustration down the line.

That's an excellent model for managers in search of a sound strategy for solving problems.

If you're going to think like a scientist as you confront problems, you need to adopt a careful, disciplined, logical system to guide your analysis. The material presented in this chapter provides a blueprint for shoving emotions aside and evaluating verifiable information in an efficient and solution-oriented manner.

Accepting the Problem

The temptation to deny, dismiss, or disregard problems can prove overwhelming to a busy manager. If you're racing around all day putting out fires, you may simply shut down rather than accept that there's something else wrong that needs your attention.

We all have only a finite amount of energy to devote to work. And we're blessed—or cursed—with a selective attention span. That leaves us vulnerable to blocking out bad news. Even worse, we might resort to outrage or vexation rather than confront the issue at hand.

Admitting that a problem exists doesn't mean you need an instant strategy to deal with it. You may have no idea what to do or where to turn for help. Yet recognizing the situation in stark, clear-headed terms is in itself a vital first step.

Some managers prefer to wait to acknowledge a problem rather than overreact too soon. "Things go wrong all the time," a general manager of a shopping mall told me. "Quite often I find that what looks like a problem on Monday can die on its own accord by Friday without my having to lift a finger."

The Devil's in the Denial   ⚠️ CAUTION!

If you react to problems by denying their seriousness and refusing to learn more, you're going to pay a high price later. Here are some clues that you're closing yourself off from the problem:

- You say or think, "Oh, that's nothing," despite evidence that something serious is amiss.
- You say or think, "I can't believe it!" without digging for more information.
- You cover your ears and say, "I don't want to hear another word!"
- You find fault with the messenger ("He doesn't know what he's talking about" or "She's just an alarmist") rather than analyze the message.

That's true on occasion, but don't bank on it.

Assuming that a problem will fade away by itself leaves you in a weak position if it doesn't. Adversity may strike in waves as one problem morphs into another. The tendency for multiple outbreaks to occur, as discussed in Chapter 2, can ignite a tiny flame of a problem into a raging fire.

An even riskier approach is to rationalize a problem to the point where it seems entirely normal, harmless, and unthreatening. You might label a miscue as a "cost of doing business" or view a vendor dispute with ho-hum apathy. If a boss were to ask you point-blank, "Is this a problem?" you would laugh and say, "Of course not."

By refusing to accept what's wrong, however, you wind up assuming a false sense of security. What you deem normal may strike your colleagues as worrisome or damaging to your business. The ability to face facts in an unbiased frame of mind helps you make more sensible decisions and set in motion effective solutions.

Writing a Problem Summary

Henry knew he had a problem. His employees didn't comply with safety regulations in his plant, resulting in an above-average number of injuries and a higher worker's compensation premium. He realized that, unless he took action, more people would get hurt. Henry didn't want to strong-arm employees with threats of fines and other penalties, but at the same time he feared that lax enforcement of safety rules would make workers complacent.

To his credit, Henry didn't run from the problem. He could've thought, "Oh, these things go in cycles. I'm sure our safety record will improve. We'll have good years and bad years."

Better yet, he didn't react emotionally. He skipped the fretting ("What will the CEO think of me?") and the self-flagellation ("How did I get stuck with such dolts for employees? Where did I go wrong?").

Henry wisely opted to confront the problem head on. Like a scientist preparing to conduct research, he defined his purpose and mission. Then he set about seeking answers. He wrote a summary of the problem as he understood it:

> The injury rate of employees has increased in the last year, largely due to violations of safety procedures. Workers know the rules, but often ignore them or only partially comply. We need to educate employees about safety and make sure they follow the regulations.

Armed with that description of the problem, Henry enlisted the help of coworkers and employees on seeking solutions. He discussed the safety hazards with them in person, but he also distributed his written problem summary to ensure everyone understood the core issue.

> **Key Term**
>
> **Problem summary** A written characterization of a problem provides an overview of what's wrong and what must happen for the situation to improve. It's usually limited to 50 words and captures the most important aspect of a problem along with the cause and the solution.

As you wrap your mind around a problem, the trick is to communicate it to yourself—and others—concisely and coherently. Describe the situation in a neutral, accurate, and precise tone. Writing it down enables you to detach yourself and assess the issue from a healthy distance.

Managers often tell me that simply by rereading the first draft of their problem summary, they make headway toward finding solutions. They may see it in a different light because they're reading it rather than worrying about it. And they can communicate the problem to others in an unbiased, consistent way by submitting it in writing.

If you lack confidence in your writing ability, don't let that stop you. No one's grading your work. The objective isn't to compose perfect prose, but to express the issue on paper so that it's characterized clearly.

The first few times you write problem summaries, you may find it hard to resist injecting your opinion into your description. In fact, managers often report that they experience a rush of anxiety when they try to encapsulate the challenge they face in print.

"I got a little upset having to write out what was already a pretty nasty situation," a supervisor said. "It made me resent the folks who I thought were responsible for getting us into this mess. I kept thinking, 'I hate this.' And because I'm not someone who likes to write things down, that made the whole thing that much more uncomfortable for me."

With practice, this supervisor found it easier to jot problem summaries. Today she waits until she's just about to leave the office to do her writing, when she's tired and eager to "cut right to the chase and get home."

Labeling the Cause

The problems that managers face come in all shapes and sizes. But even though the facts may differ each time, workplace challenges tend to fall loosely into one of three general categories. Knowing what's causing the conflict can help you decide how to solve it.

I Want but I Can't Have

A big part of any manager's job is to set goals and reach them. Yet as hard as you work, what you want to achieve often proves elusive or downright impossible. You may lack the budget, staff, or knowledge to move from A to B and attain the objectives set by you or your boss. There's almost nothing more frustrating to a manager than knowing what you must do to succeed but lacking the tools or resources to get there.

This kind of problem boils down to "I want ... but I can't have."

Rookie managers tend to respond to these situations by either trying to impose their will on others ("I want you to work harder and smarter, so *do it!*") or backing down. Neither approach bears fruit.

> ### Replace "I Want" with "You Want"
> Rather than make "I want" statements, think in terms of your peers' or employees' interests. Analyze the problem from their perspective with "You want" statements. For example, replace "I want you to sacrifice for the team" with "You want to prove your value as a leader and reach higher goals." When you show that you appreciate others' viewpoints and you label the problem as they see it, they'll lower their guard and be more willing to make concessions. Best of all, they'll see you as an empathetic ally rather than a tyrannical boss.

If your problem fits the "I want but I can't have" mold, stop thinking in negative terms. Consider what you *can* have—what's possible—with the cooperation of others. Granted, you may not be able to march unilaterally toward an entirely satisfying solution. But at least you can make the most of compromise and negotiate a middle ground that offers partial victory without jeopardizing your relationships with employees.

It's Not My Fault

When a problem erupts in the workplace, the blame police are often the first to arrive on the scene. Your boss wants to know "who screwed up." Team members mutter that they "knew this would happen" but couldn't stop it. Others shrug and take no responsibility for the mess.

That leaves you holding the bag.

You want to grab a megaphone and tell everyone, "It's not *my* fault!" But you're the manager. You're in charge. All fingers point to you and your reputation's on the line.

Adopt a defensive stance and you'll incriminate yourself. Claiming that "I was just following instructions" or "I made the best decision I could with the information available to me" won't save you. In fact, trying to justify your actions by subtly shifting blame to others can squander whatever credibility you still retain.

It's better to raise the discussion to another plane. Rather than debate who's to blame, wear a scientist's hat. Study what happened, why it happened, and what to do next.

Remove faultfinding from your attempt to solve problems.

Narrate the Event

Smart Managing   Give an account of what happened as if you're filing a police report. Keep personalities out of it and refrain from judgments. Simply describe the sequence of events, step by step. Imagine each sentence as beginning with "Here's what happened next..." Use phrasing such as "At this point, I determined something was wrong and I discovered that..." or "This information led me to...." That's better than saying, "That's when I sensed someone had made a mistake and I discovered that..." or "I finally got the information even though it should've been sent to me sooner and it led me to...."

Raising issues of blame will block your ability to gather facts, assess the situation, and develop solutions. Imagine you're in a laboratory analyzing the problem from a safe distance—and you're determined to uncover the truth and learn from it.

The Either/or Bind

There are usually more than two roads that lead away from a problem. But besieged managers may assume that they only have two choices: either A or B.

Experienced scientists research a problem by considering all types of solutions. They do not get locked into narrow either/or thinking. By taking a broader, more sweeping perspective, they're able to assess their options with open minds.

Beware of naysayers who impose an either/or construct on your situation. Even well-intentioned bosses or mentors might wind up making matters worse by presenting you with a Hobson's choice: you may think you're choosing freely when in fact you lack any feasible alternatives.

Kevin, a retail manager, faced this dilemma when he told his boss he accidentally ordered $5,000 of the wrong product from a supplier. Both of them knew it was too late to cancel the order.

"Either you convince the supplier to accept a return," Kevin's boss said, "or it's coming out of your pocket."

Since Kevin knew the supplier never accepted returns and stated this no-return policy in big bold print on every order form, that left the "choice" of owing his employer $5,000. But he analyzed the situation as if it were a brainteaser. He said to himself, "I've got $5,000 worth of goods on order. I don't want them. We can't sell them to our customers. I can't return them. But I'm not going to pay for them out of my pocket. What are some other solutions?"

That's when Kevin realized he could sell the goods to another retailer. So he negotiated a deal to transfer the shipment to an interested party that paid him nearly $5,000. By treating the problem as a puzzle to solve, Kevin found a way out. He didn't lament his mistake ("How could I be so dumb?") or panic over his boss's threat ("I can't afford to cough up $5,000!"). He kept calm, searched for alternatives, and found one that clicked.

No BMWs Allowed Here

Smart managers ration their emotional outbursts. They get carried away only when they want to make an especially memorable impact on their workers. Just as lab researchers don't rant and rave when an experiment goes awry, mature supervisors limit their range of emotional expressiveness so that it doesn't detract from speedy problem solving.

By setting a levelheaded example and digesting problems with calm clarity, wise managers model for their employees how to respond to setbacks. Hopefully, staffers will follow their boss's lead and skip the emotional torment when they confront difficulties head on.

Cut the Complaining!

In *Control Your Destiny or Someone Else Will* by Noel M. Tichy and Stratford Sherman (revised, New York: HarperBusiness, 2001, p. 142), the authors describe how Jack Welch, the former CEO of General Electric, responded to grousing by his managers after financial wrongdoing was discovered in the firm's defense unit. GE managers complained to Welch, "When are we going to get the government off our backs?" He replied, "You've lost your right to *not* have the government on your back. The system failed, there was dishonesty, and both the government and GE will stay on your back until we clean up this mess."

But some people never learn.

If you manage more than 10 people, you'll probably wind up with at least one "BMW"—an individual who *bitches, moans,* and *whines* rather than bear down and produce results. Left unchecked, this behavior can spread like a virus. An entire team can soon drown in negative emotions.

Shut down complainers in their tracks. Insist that everyone focus on the facts, fix what's broken, and develop a long-term strategy to avoid a recurrence of the problem. Marching around the office throwing fits or shifting into BMW mode will signal to your employees that it's fine for them to drop everything and join the gripe chorus.

Frustrated employees can work themselves into a tizzy as they commiserate over a problem. They can engage in woe-is-me pity-mongering or fling accusations at the nearest convenient target. Some managers permit such behavior under the misguided notion that it'll blow over. Or they might rationalize that people bond and gain comfort from each other when they can complain freely about a problem. In reality, however, complaining begets more complaining. No one wins and nothing's accomplished.

Another technique to shut down malcontents is to draw the line on what they can and cannot control. Literally. Respond to an employee's tirade by calling the person aside and conducting a simple exercise. Take a sheet of paper and create two

Take the Hit

If you can't cure chronic complainers, at least make sure they're not contagious. Hold one-on-one meetings with them to review their performance. If they grumble and lash out, soak up their griping with equanimity. Allow them to unload their negative feelings before expecting them to quiet down. Acknowledge their concerns and then change the subject.

While you may dread such encounters, it's better for you to take the hit than to let complainers dump their irritation on hapless coworkers. Absorb most if not all of their hostility and they'll be less likely to foment rebellion or demotivate their peers.

columns with the headings "Control" and "Can't Control." As the employee indulges in BMW antics, take notes. List each grievance in the appropriate column based on whether the issue is within the employee's control or beyond it.

By creating an at-a-glance summary of workers' perceived problems—and separating the ones within their control from those that cannot be helped—you enable them to distinguish between issues they should address and those they should let go. It's an unemotional way of saying, "Stop the griping and start solving problems."

Analyze This—Then Judge It

Arthur C. Martinez, the former chairman and CEO of Sears, Roebuck & Co., can speak with intense, heartfelt emotion when the occasion calls for it. But most of the time, he's a dry-eyed realist who thinks through decisions with scientific precision.

He ran Sears for most of the 1990s and faced huge problems. When he took charge in 1992, he confronted a massively bureaucratic corporate behemoth that was losing $4 billion. By 1994, he had turned the company around and ensured its survival. But that meant shutting down the popular Sears catalog, which was losing $150 million a year.

Martinez tackled the problem of what to do with the catalog business the same way he addressed countless other management challenges—by adopting a calm, systematic decision-making process.

"When you face big problems, you need to decide what to do by getting all the facts as rapidly as possible and avoiding prejudgment," Martinez told me. "Begin with your analysis, which must be very clear, free of emotion, and based on reasonable assumptions and valid information. But the analytic portion is only one element in problem solving. The second and final step is to apply your judgment."

In grappling with what to do with a money-losing but venerated retail catalog, Martinez analyzed the problem by asking himself questions such as "Do we have a clear plan?" "What's the execution risk of that plan?" "Are we making reasonable assumptions?" and "Can we fix this problem within our tight time frame?"

Once he worked with his management team to assemble thorough answers to these questions, he evaluated what to do. Here's where emotion entered the equation, because he knew that closing the catalog would cause massive layoffs. In the end, he decided that Sears couldn't pull off a turnaround in its catalog and its retail stores at once. To survive as a company, he concluded that Sears must focus all its attention on improving its stores' performance.

As soon as you confront a problem, cleanse your mind of all preconceptions of what will solve it. Expose yourself to limitless possibilities—at least for now—as you dissect the issue and amass verifiable information.

Consider how basketball legend Lenny Wilkens responded when head coach Chuck Daly asked him to serve as an assis-

A Time to Judge

TOOLS Before you judge how to fix a problem, you need to analyze it from every angle. This sounds simple, but you may find it hard not to prejudge and let your biases interfere. Complete this questionnaire to guide your analysis of a particular problem:

1. Can I clearly define the primary cause of the problem?
2. Is there general agreement among my colleagues that this problem exists and merits attention?
3. Will the problem continue or intensify if I do nothing?
4. Are there actions I can take to eliminate or mitigate the problem?
5. Can I enlist the help of others?
6. Can I collect all the information I need to understand the problem?

If you answered "Yes" to all the questions, you're ready to proceed to the next step and judge what to do. This involves weighing risks and rewards of each potential solution and evaluating the likelihood that you'll achieve the objective you've set.

If you answered "No" to any of the questions, that indicates you must remove stumbling blocks to make progress. You may need to gather more facts or persuade key allies to assist you before you choose an action plan and gauge your odds of success.

tant on the Olympic "Dream Team" in 1992. Wilkens felt he deserved to be head coach; furthermore, he suspected that Daley offered him the assistant coach spot because he's black and his pairing with Daly, who's white, would provide "racial balance" (*Investor's Business Daily*, January 9, 2001, p. A4).

While disappointed, Wilkens didn't act rashly. He analyzed the situation, gathered more facts, and decided to accept the job. Smart move. Four years later, he earned the chance to become head coach on the Olympic "Dream Team II"—and his squad won the gold medal.

Withholding your judgment until after you've completed a rigorous analysis protects you from rash, emotionally driven actions. You'll find that, like Arthur Martinez, you can make the hardest, most high-stakes decisions free from bias. While 100% objectivity is an elusive goal, you'll find that thinking like a fact-finding, curious scientist raises your awareness so that you're ready to call the right shots.

Manager's Checklist for Chapter 7

❑ Upon discovering a problem, skip right to gathering information and assessing it. Don't berate yourself or get too emotional.

❑ Accept that a problem exists, even if you have no idea what to do about it.

❑ Write a statement of a problem that describes what's wrong and what must happen in order to reach a solution.

❑ Characterize a problem based on what *others* want, such as your employees, customers, and bosses. Understand how they view the situation and what outcomes they prefer.

❑ Resist either/or thinking in favor of a more flexible, creative search for solutions.

❑ Silence complainers by insisting they focus on investigating the facts and proposing action steps.

❑ Wait to judge what to do until after you've fully analyzed a problem with an open mind.

Problem-Solvers vs. Problem-Creators

E very manager confronts problems. But for some poor souls, the problems never seem to stop.

A proactive, problem-solving attitude prevents you from drowning in mishaps. By acting decisively and looking for ways to mitigate the damage, you contain the fallout. But by reacting with self-pity, anger, or resentment, you prolong the agony and breed a hapless, disaster-prone approach to workaday pressures.

"You can find problems everywhere when you start looking," says Kenneth Gergen, a Swarthmore College psychology professor (*Harvard Management Communication Letter*, October 2001, p. 5). "If you take it too far, you create a sense that it's all insurmountable. But if [you] could construct a world in which something is possible…you create a tremendous positive energy."

Thinking in terms of "What's possible?" rather than "Why me?" focuses your attention on solutions. It's the difference between taking a setback in stride and allowing it to overtake you. It distinguishes problem-solvers—the people who act boldly and bravely to rise above potentially debilitating challenges—from "problem-creators"—the folks who sigh their way through the workday, acting halfheartedly or turning passive when they can least afford to. Their inability to think clearly, adopt a positive attitude, and take prudent action almost guarantees that they'll become a magnet for attracting problems.

Vive la Différence!

Problem-solvers:
- respond to problems with alacrity
- are energized by sampling solutions
- keep their perspective in tough times
- look ahead with optimism
- enlist allies to help fix what's broken
- exert discipline to finish what they start
- learn from their mistakes

Problem-creators:
- react to problems with dread
- are exhausted by all that's wrong
- blow mishaps out of proportion
- assume one problem leads to another
- label others "useless" or "part of the problem"
- give up after making a token effort
- repeat the same mistakes

What separates problem-solvers from problem-creators is self-confidence, a core belief that "I can deal with this" as opposed to "I'm helpless." Events can conspire against you, but it's up to you whether you allow them to pummel you into submission.

Four Problem-Creation Traps

In my seminars, I'll meet many managers who scratch their heads and say, "You know, it's just one problem after another where I work." When we discuss the details, it's often apparent to me that these individuals bring much of their woe upon themselves needlessly.

Here are the four most common traps that these problem-addled managers face.

1. **Failure to manage poor performers.** It sounds heartless, but here goes: *To survive and succeed, managers must develop a*

consistent and often brutal strategy to deal with the least effective workers. Ignoring or rationalizing lazy, inept, or otherwise shoddy employees is like pinning a sign on your back that reads, "Hit me. I deserve it."

In *The War for Talent* (Boston: Harvard Business School Press, 2001), McKinsey & Company consultants Ed Michaels, Helen Handfield-Jones, and Beth Axelrod urge organizations to address the problem of "C players"—whom they define as the bottom 10% to 20% of the workforce—either by training them to boost their performance or removing them from their jobs. Left unchecked, these ineffectual workers not only harm productivity and gum the operations, but also block advancement opportunities for stronger, more deserving performers. What's worse, managers spend so much time on poor performers that they neglect their other staffers. And fewer stars—the "A players"— want to be with a company that demonstrates a high tolerance for duds.

2. Refusal to praise employees. It's no secret that the quickest way to become a beloved boss is to recognize employees' efforts. Yet even though almost every manager understands the critical role of praise, getting in the habit of saying "Good job" or "Well done" seems an almost Herculean task for problem-creators.

When I led workshops for a financial services company, everyone griped about a manager who never acknowledged, much less praised, his employees' work. The manager, in turn, told me he hated his job and said, "Every day I walk in here and I'm greeted with problems." Yet once he committed to praising his team members more regularly—and followed through—he found they showed more initiative and extinguished fires before they raged out of control.

3. Abuse of the truth. As a manager, your days are numbered if you get a reputation for fudging the truth. Maybe you can survive a few years if you're surrounded by equally dissembling peers and bosses. But your chance of long-term survival is nil.

Underpromise, Overdeliver

Tone down the sweeping promises you make to your staff, especially if fulfilling a commitment isn't entirely within your control. Limit use of phrases such as "I absolutely guarantee that" or "Rest assured you'll never have to worry about that." When speculating about the future, leave some wiggle room to respond to changing circumstances. If you tell an employee, "I'll stand by you through thick and thin," that sounds nice but can invite problems if that employee subsequently violates company policy.

When I ask workers to identify their No. 1 complaint with their supervisors, the most popular answer by far is "They say one thing and then do another." So if you're the kind of person who reneges on commitments or misleads your troops, then you're sure to experience all kinds of easily avoidable problems. Employees will doubt your word, scoff at your suggestions, and interpret your promises by taking a 180-degree opposite view.

4. Misguided faith in gut instinct. The recent emphasis in business books and magazine articles on "harnessing your intuition" can wind up breeding a whole new generation of problem-creators. Managers who use their hunches or instincts as an excuse for gathering facts and examining them rigorously will double or even triple the number of on-the-job problems they encounter. It's not that your intuition is wrong or that your gut will mislead you, but many managers concentrate so intently on internal feelings that they willfully disregard external events.

Strike a sensible middle ground. To think like a

Use the 90/10 Formula

When pondering a problem, watch the clock. Spend about 90% of your time collecting information, confirming the facts, and investigating options. Allot the other 10% of the time you devote to problem solving to plumbing the physical and nonphysical sensations, hunches, and insights that help guide you. But beware: you can experience flashes of intuition when you least expect them. If you're digging for gut feelings and getting nowhere, take a short walk or surf the Web mindlessly for a few minutes and let the messages trickle in.

problem-solver, combine an exhaustive analysis of the situation with an awareness of your gut feelings. Study a problem from all angles, ask the right questions of the right people, and invest time in researching and sampling possible solutions. Then, before you set in motion your solution steps, make sure it "feels right" inside.

Managing Your Mouth

Problem-solvers think before they talk. When they're facilitating personnel disputes, they're tactful, fair, and eager to treat all parties with dignity.

Problem-creators, by contrast, talk themselves into trouble. They gab too much, fling careless accusations, or contradict themselves—or others—to the point where their comments either come back to haunt them or turn to gibberish.

If you're gregarious by nature, you might not perceive your chattiness as a liability. You may come to believe, perhaps rightly, that most people love your personality and hang breathlessly on your every word. The danger arises when you let your mouth run freely. Even the most stimulating speakers risk boring their listeners or accidentally alienating them by saying something that's off-putting. In fact, you can regale someone for 10 minutes straight making all kinds of witty, entertaining, complimentary remarks. But if in the 11th minute you make a comment that rubs that person the wrong way, he'll probably dwell on that one little slip-up and disregard everything else you've said.

Watching what you say—and how much you say—can help you avoid problems and solve the ones you already

The Three-Second Pause

Smart Managing When you sense you're talking too much, stop when you reach the end of your next sentence. Mentally count to three. This cushion of silence gives others a chance to chime in, thus preventing you from dominating the discussion. If three seconds elapse and no one else speaks, gauge whether they seem engaged in what you're saying—or bored and apathetic. You may realize in those three seconds that you're talking yourself into oblivion, that people have already made up their minds and decided to tune out.

face. Managing your mouth is particularly important when you do any of the following three things.

When you give instructions. Pace yourself so that employees can follow every step of a process. Pepper your explanations with questions ("Does that make sense?" or "Do you want to go over that with me to make sure I said it right?") to foster a dialogue. Above all, give people a chance to show they're willing and able to comply with your directions. You'll save yourself from big problems simply by letting employees voice concerns, ask questions, and clarify their confusion before you rush off.

A problem-creator dumps too much information on a frazzled worker, flees, and then remains inaccessible for days while the employee guesses what to do next. Making too many "do this/do that" demands while talking nonstop also increases the odds that resentful staffers will rebel.

When you handle conflict. Problem-solvers listen for mutual understanding. They make sure all parties appreciate each other's views before they try to resolve the conflict. That requires lots of gentle prodding ("Jim, what do you think Mark wants? How does he see this?") so that individuals empathize and embrace a broader perspective.

Problem-creators react to conflicts by making snap judgments and picking sides. They give too many commands ("Jim, stop that!" or "Mark, you're not being fair") and inflame tensions among bickering employees.

When you respond to gossip. If you're going to memorize one equation relating to management survival, try this one: *gossip = problems.*

In your eagerness to forge bonds with peers and employees, you might treat gossip as harmless or even fun. But as much as you want to win friends and allies on the job, passing or receiving gossip won't help. It creates a dynamic where you know something about others that taints your perception of them and prevents you from assessing people or situations in an unbiased, balanced light.

> **⚠ CAUTION!**
>
> ### Etched in Stone
>
> From my experience counseling managers on solving problems, I've found that motormouths tend to confront more people problems than reserved personalities. Why? Spoken words cannot be deleted—and they often remain in the memory. When you're writing, you can craft your words to convey your precise meaning, but when you're talking, what comes out first is what lasts. It amazes me how some employees will never forget a manager's single, seemingly innocent crack or caustic put-down from long ago, even after years of reporting to this otherwise decent boss.

Problem-solvers instinctively turn away from gossip. They honor Grandma's advice, "If you don't have something nice to say about someone, don't say anything at all." And they live by the addendum, "If you hear others say something that's not nice about someone, don't listen."

Difficult? Or Just Different?

Hank couldn't take it anymore. After five years of managing a health care center, he barely hid his disdain for nurses: "They have no loyalty!" "They're just gimme, gimme, gimme," "Getting them to stop complaining and start working is a triumph in itself."

Naturally, Hank's days were chaotic and filled with problems. A classic problem-creator, he allowed his frustration with nurses to interfere with his ability to manage his business effectively. Instead of maintaining an air of professionalism (even if he was stewing inside), he displayed open hostility to the very people he relied upon to provide care to his center's patients.

"Hank, regardless of how you feel about nurses, you're only making things worse on yourself by repeatedly insulting them," I told him. "That breeds ill will, an environment that's ideal for spawning problems."

Like Hank, problem-solvers face their share of run-ins with employees. But unlike Hank, they skip the tirades and focus on finding ways to get along and forge solutions. They realize that people who rub them the wrong way are more *different* than *difficult*.

Malcontent Alert!

During my college years, I took a part-time job working for a manager who would spend at least a few minutes a day pounding his desk and throwing a fit. Before I grew accustomed to his antics, I'd rush in to see if something was wrong. He'd always say the same thing, "How did I get stuck with so many malcontents!" Then he'd identify his latest "malcontent" by name and tell me how this person "needed to get with the program—or else." This manager would instantly brand as malcontents and ostracize any employees who didn't please him. Within a year, this manager was terminated.

Admitting that someone you don't especially like is different drives you to understand that person better. You attempt to bridge gaps and seek common ground rather than lash out and label them as difficult.

Thinking in terms of differences among people helps you rise above petty animosity. You save all the energy that would otherwise go to developing a grudge against someone. Better yet, you step off the "problem treadmill." Rather than scheme and speak out against a troublemaker, you figure out how to understand that person, look past clashing personalities, and work together productively.

Learning Your Lesson

Based on what you've read in this chapter, you should be fairly sure at this point whether you lean toward solving problems or creating them. If you tend to create more problems than you solve, you've gained strategies in the preceding pages on how to reform your work habits and adjust your mindset.

I've saved the most fundamental difference between problem-solvers and problem-creators for last: the ability to learn from mistakes.

Problem-solvers thirst for knowledge. They're always looking for ways to improve, for techniques that give them an edge in minimizing or eliminating future problems. Problem-creators curse their lot in life and ricochet from roadblock to roadblock. They lack the fortitude to step back, identify what's at the root of their troubles, and address it head on.

Learned helplessness A theory put forward by psychologist Martin Seligman that the experience of being in a position in which it's impossible to escape harm or pain can lead to a feeling of fatalism and resignation, a belief that there's no point in trying to improve the situation. The term is used more generally to describe a feeling of powerlessness.

Seligman described managers who adopt a passive, powerless attitude about their work as lapsing in a state of "learned helplessness." Rather than take the initiative to solve problems, they do nothing and let mishaps degenerate into crises. For Seligman, managers embrace learned helplessness because they were punished or otherwise harmed when they took a proactive stance in the past, so now they're convinced any problem-solving steps they take will fail. As a result, they sit idly and allow fresh fires to flare up all around them.

"There are many approaches we can take to solving our problems, but most of us approach them with the attitude that they are adversaries or enemies that need to be defeated or controlled, rather than seeing them as opportunities for learning and improvement," say Kenneth Cloke and Joan Goldsmith, co-authors of *Resolving Conflicts at Work* (San Francisco: Jossey-Bass, 2001), in *Harvard Management Communication Letter* (December 2001, p. 4). "We face problems all our lives, but only rarely do we stop to consider how we can improve the way we go about trying to solve them."

The ability to learn from problems gives you a head start in fixing them. If you're unwilling or unable to understand the underlying conflict and act quickly to address it, then you can fall into a tense, unproductive stalemate.

Annette Simmons, an author and management consultant, likes to tell managers a story about her dog to encourage them to think like practical problem-solvers. "When my dog's on a leash and walks on one side of the telephone pole and I walk on the other, we're not going anywhere," she'll say. "It's not until I back off that he's going to back off."

Problem-creators often refuse to back off. Even if they've been burned in the past for allowing their stubbornness to trump their better judgment, they may still fall into the same destructive pattern. Problem-solvers, by contrast, never miss a chance to learn from experience.

Seeing the Future

Gather 10 people in a room. Ask them to predict how their careers will evolve over the next year, how much they'll earn, what highlights they'll enjoy, and how their current problems will turn out.

It's a good bet that those who give inspiring, enthusiastic answers are problem-solvers, while the worrywarts are problem-creators. Anticipating your future can fill you with excitement and eagerness—or induce fear. Individuals who look ahead with hope and optimism tend to skip breezily over bumps in the road rather than trip and fall.

Many psychologists believe that fear of the future leads otherwise competent managers to see problems that don't necessarily exist. These fretful types react to signs of trouble with doubt and negativity.

I recall a supervisor, Lizzie, who flinched when her boss said, "Over the next six months or year, we're all going to have to make some sacrifices until the economy improves." Lizzie reeled in fright. She told me that she was sure she'd get a demotion and be forced to terminate her best staffers. In fact, such dark outcomes were highly unlikely. But Lizzie's "fear response" drove her into a tailspin of gloom-and-doom anxieties.

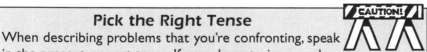

Pick the Right Tense

When describing problems that you're confronting, speak in the present or past tense. If you characterize a problem in the future tense (e.g., "We're going to be in deep trouble," "This will backfire soon enough," "I won't get the credit for that project if I take it on"), you risk making matters worse. Why? After adopting a wait-and-see-how-bad-it-gets attitude, you'll want to prove yourself "right." And that will lead you—consciously or unconsciously—to create conditions for new problems to break out.

Problem-creators feel fear even when there's no trace of actual danger. Their steadily escalating jitters warp their sense of reality. Rather than cope with the underlying source of the fear, they wind up succumbing to it. That can lead to a kind of problem-solving paralysis in which they just hunker down for a disastrous future, instead of plotting bold, creative solutions.

When you see the future, you're conjuring an image or idea. Problem-creators scare themselves with a self-defeating image or a terrible idea. That, in turn, provokes a fear response. They withdraw from teams, perceive threats that don't exist, or ignore sound advice from their boss or mentor.

When you predict the course of events in your workplace over the next few months, analyze to what extent you base your projections on fear or facts. Beware of letting the following four anxieties interfere with your ability to respond to setbacks.

Fear of failure. It's common to ponder mistakes you might make that will lead to problems. Admitting you're afraid is healthy. Problem-solvers harness that fear and use it to prepare properly for challenges, empathize with others, and anticipate and disarm conflicts before they occur. Problem-creators think, "I'll definitely mess up." Then they go through the motions with an air of dark certainty as they wait for their personal Armageddon to unfold. Or they might imagine making one error, which leads to another ... and then another ... until they've wrapped themselves in negativity.

Fear of inadequacy. Managers who doubt their experience, expertise, or character can fear an embarrassing future where they're exposed as weak or incompetent. Soon they start acting that way! They badmouth coworkers behind their backs, nod and smile robotically whenever the president enters the room, and wait to state an opinion until they're sure it won't rock the boat. Problem-solvers may share the same doubts, but they look ahead with excitement. They figure that they might as well listen closely to others, fill gaps in their knowledge, repair personality defects, and accept their self-perceived inadequacies without a fuss.

Fear of intimidation. For problem-creators, everyone's a critic. When they look to the future, they see their peers, employees, and higher-ups mercilessly judging them with increasing harshness. This leaves them feeling scared, vulnerable, and subject to ridicule. They may even talk themselves into making blunders in order to give their colleagues something to attack. Realistically, of course, most people who work around you aren't bullies. They don't judge your every move or perhaps even give you that much thought. Problem-solvers realize this.

Fear of risk. Solving a problem means taking a risk: you choose a course of action and gamble that the outcome will meet or exceed your expectations. Problem-creators often recoil from risk. They prefer to step aside and watch while others assume leadership roles. They dread a future fraught with high-stakes decisions that can make or break them. The prospect of placing bets frightens them because they lack confidence in themselves. Because they cannot foresee a time when they're able to manage necessary risk-taking, they reconcile themselves to a future filled with more problems.

Good News, Bad News

Just as problem-solvers tend to look on the bright side and allay their fears, they also use positive language that reflects their fundamental optimism. Their tendency to lace their speech with mood-enhancing words and phrases enables them to fight problems with a resilient, uplifting attitude.

Compare how a problem-solver and problem-creator express the same points:

Problem-solvers:
- "I'm happy to help you."
- "You did a great job."
- "Let's take this one step at a time."
- "This isn't working out as well as it could."
- "Let's see what we can learn from this."

Problem-creators:
- "Stop it. Let me do that."
- "That's good, but the real test is next time."
- "I don't know where to begin."
- "You're not working out for us."
- "What a screwed-up mess!"
- "We're not getting anywhere."

Problem-solvers:
- "We can work around this impasse."
- "There's a way out of this."
- "We're not out of the woods yet."

Problem-creators:
- "You better figure out what to do, pronto!"
- "We're still stuck."

By adopting a diplomatic tone, you make everyone less defensive and foster a more trusting environment for finding solutions. Employees want to work for a can-do problem-solver, a leader who's willing to state what's possible rather than what's impossible. Problem-creators use words like a stick to poke their listeners; such aggressiveness triggers antagonism and makes teamwork that much more difficult to achieve.

Delivering bad news puts even the savviest problem-solvers to the test. Describe a dire situation in clear, concise terms. Resist indulging in defeatist or alarmist statements ("We're so deep in the muck we'll be lucky to ever shake ourselves clean," "Maybe it's better if we bail out and let the ship sink," "This is just the worst!"). Take stock of the situation and place it in the proper context. End with a ray of hope, not a devastating downer.

Communicate like a problem-solver and you'll find that everyone within earshot follows your lead. They'll stare down crises with the same steely resolve that you show. Your positive language will not only help you survive the toughest times, but it will enhance your stature as a leader who can withstand the heat and lead even the most disheartened employees to overcome their problems and their attitudes.

Manager's Checklist for Chapter 8

❑ Think in terms of "What's possible?" rather than "Why me?" when you respond to problems.

❑ Act fast to manage poor performers. Once you identify the bottom 10% or 20% of your employees, train them to improve their performance or remove them from their jobs.

❏ Avoid promising too much to your staff, especially if fulfilling your commitment isn't entirely within your control. Replace "I absolutely guarantee that…" with "It's highly likely that…."

❏ Unplug your motormouth. Silently count to three after you complete a sentence so that others can get a word in.

❏ When you train employees, let them voice concerns, ask questions, and clarify their confusion every step of the way. Avoid issuing "do this/do that" demands.

❏ Resolve conflicts by helping all parties to understand each other's views. That's better than judging too soon and taking sides.

❏ View people who rub you the wrong way as *different,* not *difficult.*

❏ Make sound predictions based on facts and optimism, not fear and pessimism.

Combating the Threat of Change

In the 1970s, you couldn't find a book on managing change. Now there are dozens of titles on this topic. Over the last two decades, massive upheavals have jolted the conventional, hierarchical, orderly work world. And that leaves many of us shaken and unsure what to do next.

Change blankets today's workplace. CEOs routinely say, "The one constant in our business is change." Business school professors lecture about it, consultants run workshops on it, yet most employees still dread it.

That's where you fit in.

Your survival as a manager largely depends on your ability to weather change, through developing a flexible attitude about your own projects and rallying your team members to persevere despite twists and turns that threaten to derail them. Finding sensible ways to cope with change helps you deal with all kinds of problems, from process breakdowns to interpersonal conflicts. Experience teaches you to anticipate and prepare for disruptions.

With all the evolution-
ary turmoil that has
wracked organizations in
recent years, the irony is
the vast number of
"change survivors" who
remain in their jobs—"cyn-
ical people who've learned
how to live through change
programs without really
changing at all" (Jeanie
Daniel Duck, "Managing
Change: The Art of
Balancing," *Harvard
Business Review*, November-December 1993, pp. 111-112).

> **Paradigm shift** A meta-
> morphosis from one mode
> of behaving and thinking into
> another. It's caused by a confluence of
> forces and results in a collective
> change in attitude. The spread of e-
> mail, for instance, has ushered in a
> paradigm shift in how people com-
> municate. The term was popularized
> by Thomas S. Kuhn, the late philoso-
> pher of science, in his classic book,
> *The Structure of Scientific Revolutions*
> (Chicago: University of Chicago
> Press, 1962).

Managing these individuals takes a mixed bag of skills. You
need to communicate early and often about potential changes,
serve as a sounding board for frustrated or anxious workers in
need of reassurance, and maintain everyone's focus when
they'd rather stay home or commiserate in the cafeteria.

Three Myths of Managing Change

Despite all the attention paid to change, misconceptions
abound. Managers might accept certain "truths," only to learn
from the problems that erupt in their unit that reality doesn't fit
their preconceptions.

Lead your team more effectively by separating myth from
reality. Beware of three of the most commonly held beliefs
about change that can fool you into making the wrong moves.

Myth 1: Employees Will Fight Change

You assume that your workers will oppose change, because
conventional wisdom teaches you that people cling to a calm,
predictable status quo. That's true for a handful of hardcore
resistants. But the majority of people in any 21st-century company know that we live in an age of speed where CEOs can

Show Them What They've Got

TRICKS OF THE TRADE

Prepare your employees to respond well to organizational change. How? Point out how they're already doing a great job as change agents, even if they don't see themselves that way. Praise them for modifying their work routines, suggesting an idea to improve productivity, developing a new skill, or enrolling in a night class to earn a degree or professional designation. Recast such actions as evidence of their openness to change and eagerness to fight complacency. Once you help them appreciate the strengths they already exhibit, they'll gain the confidence to accept more sweeping changes.

come and go overnight, cubicles can be reconfigured in a few hours, and entire divisions of a firm can get bought, sold, and reacquired all within a few months.

Some researchers argue that human beings are conditioned from birth to incorporate change into their lives. Our bodies develop and grow. Our moods swing from moment to moment. Our skills, friends, and beliefs change. We job-hop an average of seven or eight times in our careers, we relocate for both personal and professional reasons, and roughly half of us who marry will divorce. If we hated change all that much, we would refashion our lives to make them more stable and simple.

Even a seemingly jolting change can lift our spirits. Consider the most insecure workers who cling to their jobs despite a history of poor performance reviews. They seem to fear change and want nothing more than to be left alone, right? Not necessarily. If you call them into your office and either terminate them or offer them another position more suited to their abilities, they may heave a sigh of relief and leave the meeting with a new lease on life.

Myth 2: Change Means Something's Wrong

Employees see through the spin. When the CEO announces a wrenching change but insists that "it's for everyone's good," no one believes it.

Yet that doesn't mean workers automatically hit the panic button whenever they learn of a change. If the company relocates its offices or replaces a few senior executives, employees may cheer.

"In the days before we let the staff know that we were overhauling our business plan and shutting down our e-commerce unit, I feared they might quit in droves," a business owner told me. "I figured they would lose faith in our leadership. But as it turns out, some of them actually applauded when we made the announcement! They couldn't be happier with us for finally taking action."

When you inform your staff of changes, level with them. Deliver the facts straight up. Allow them to judge the change on its own merits. Don't assume they'll read between the lines and conclude there's more trouble afoot.

The danger of believing this myth is it can lead you to strike a defensive tone. You might go out of your way to reassure employees that the change doesn't bode ill for the company's future or reveal an underlying problem. The more you keep insisting that everything's fine, the more your employees may wonder why you're belaboring the point.

Myth 3: Change Causes Stress

Stress exists with or without change. It ebbs and flows daily based on dozens of variables. Granted, change can disrupt employees' normal rhythms and trigger anxiety and short tempers. But the underlying cause of stress usually stems from deadening work, unreasonable demands, unrealistic performance standards, or personality clashes. Change itself may exacerbate such tensions, but it's rarely the primary cause.

Believing this myth can lead you to take missteps when managing your staff. You may misdiagnose their stress as an outgrowth of organizational change and thus ignore the more direct factors that afflict them.

Looking Ahead in Increments

"Some changes are in store around here."
Most employees who hear that from upper management will

What's Stressing You?

When an employee appears stressed in the midst of change, find out why. Meet with him or her and review this checklist:

_____ You enjoy your work.
_____ You like the people you work with.
_____ You're caught up with all your work.
_____ You're proud to work for this organization.
_____ You understand our processes and procedures.
_____ You have all the tools and resources to do your job.
_____ You have enough hours in the day to complete your high-priority work.
_____ Your personal life is in order.

Don't expect to check every line. Almost all employees, if they're honest, will admit to at least one facet of their job that isn't satisfactory. That's a good place to start to help them tame their stress.

assume it's an understatement. They may envision a worst-case scenario with severe disruptions of work flow, massive layoffs, and yet another departmental "reorganization." The anticipatory dread that sets in can become a self-fulfilling prophecy as workers brace for all the headaches that inevitably accompany major change campaigns. This chain reaction can spawn a fresh wave of conflicts as employees gripe and worry about the painful aftereffects of change.

You can prevent this downhill spiral by communicating about change in increments. Present each development piece by piece, as bite-size chunks that employees view as manageable, not oppressive. If your organization truly faces a massive overhaul, break it down into distinct stages and focus on one at a time. This boosts everyone's morale and increases buy-in along the way.

By presenting change in digestible chunks, you reduce its perceived threat. This allows workers to wrap their minds around each set of reforms. They might still fret or disagree with what's happening, but if you maintain open lines of communication and encourage dialogue, you can establish a baseline of trust.

1-3-6

Communicate change to employees within set time frames to lower resistance and prevent problems. Follow the 1-3-6 formula:

Identify what's going to happen after *one* month, such as testing new procedures or researching ways to streamline production.

A month later, look ahead *three* months and explain what will happen, such as building on your initial findings and running cost-benefit studies to weigh more ambitious reforms.

Three months later, announce a *six*-month implementation plan. This might include the introduction of new processes or the installation of new systems.

By gradually expanding your time horizon, you can keep employees informed without overwhelming them with too much change, too soon.

Here's another advantage of taking this methodical approach: rumor control. Narrow the focus of a change to a shorter period of time and you reduce the number of unknowns that swirl around the workplace. Once employees understand each step of the change process in detail, along with its short-term objectives, they'll be less likely to question what's going on behind the scenes. Give them the answers they're seeking and they'll find less reason to tap the rumor mill.

Whenever possible, provide training to help workers adjust to change more easily. Time the training sessions to correspond with the current stage of the change campaign and you'll enable employees to apply what

The Incremental Yes

Smart Managing

To earn employees' buy-in for change, borrow a technique from top salespeople. To get a prospect to make a big commitment, shrewd salespeople may start by getting the buyer to agree to a series of smaller but gradually escalating commitments. Once someone agrees to pay $5 for a trial size, for instance, he may be willing to pay $10 for a larger size and $25 for a jumbo pack. Convince your employees to say yes to minor inconveniences or make small sacrifices. From that starting point, you can gradually ask them to accept bigger inconveniences or make more significant sacrifices.

they learn right away. This breeds confidence and makes the change seem more manageable. For example, if you're switching software providers as part of a larger system upgrade, devote a series of workshops specifically to helping employees master the new software.

When Projections Go Awry

In the midst of change, everyone wants to know the same things: *When will this end? How will this affect me? Will there be more changes?*

You want to give accurate answers, but there's a problem: you're not psychic. You can't see the future, yet all these questions require that you predict uncertain outcomes.

Managers who attempt to reassure employees during periods of upheaval can either level with their team or cheer them up with rosy forecasts. Leveling with people means telling them what you know for sure—and admitting what you don't know. It requires giving lots of "Time will tell" responses when they ask what lies ahead. That's the smart, safe, and honest approach.

Some managers prefer to predict a sunny future even if they have no idea what will happen. They figure that's the best way to lift everyone's spirits. So they wind up saying, "Everything's going to be fine," "We'll pull through this," and "It's all downhill from here." That may sound nice, but it's a high-risk strategy when you and your employees are experiencing dramatic change. If the situation deteriorates further, you can lose credibility when you need it most.

Resist the urge to engage in future-oriented happy talk. Try better ways to reassure your employees and earn their trust:

- **Share non-confidential information in a timely manner.** Rather than project what may or may not happen later, let everyone know what's happening *now*. Give frequent updates on organizational changes. Set up an intranet or use daily voice-mail recordings to pass along information quickly and efficiently to all your employees.

- **Heed employees' concerns.** Make yourself accessible when your organization undergoes disruptive changes. Find time for employees who want to express their views. Follow up when they request information or ask questions that you can't answer right away.
- **Tie the future to the present.** When employees ask about the future, shift their focus to the present. Explain what they can do now to weather the storm and persevere in the face of more disruptions. Discuss what they *can* control, such as maintaining a strong attitude and sticking together. Admit that no one knows exactly how things will turn out, but emphasize that

> ### Give "I" Predictions
>
> **TRICKS OF THE TRADE**
>
> Rather than risk making faulty or misguided projections about changes, limit the scope of your predictions. Focus on what you will do in the future—and make sure you can deliver on your commitments.
>
> For example, promise to alert employees of breaking news as soon as possible and visit field offices twice a week. Use phrases such as "I predict that no matter what happens, I will…" and "None of us knows exactly how things will turn out, but I do know I will…."

the effective actions they take today boost the odds of success tomorrow.

Celebrating Small Wins

"I look for reasons to party," declared Terry, a customer service manager. "We're always changing directions here—which can get pretty aggravating—so if I can get my people to lighten up and act silly every so often, it makes up for at least some of the hassles they have to deal with."

Change is rarely fun for employees. But give them something to cheer about and they'll grumble less.

One of the best ways to ward off problems is to inject small but frequent celebrations into the workday. Throw parties to recognize employee birthdays or anniversaries. Better yet, salute examples of exceptional effort. If you set weekly or monthly production goals, celebrate the team's ability to withstand difficult organizational changes and attain key objectives. Or throw a bash whenever one phase of a change campaign ends, such as the day everyone finishes packing boxes for a relocation or when new regulations take effect.

Lack a generous party budget? No problem. Here are examples of low-cost ways to host a team celebration:

- **TV breaks.** Bring a video of a popular sitcom and host a screening in your conference room. Gather your crew for a half-hour respite from their jobs. Fill bowls of popcorn and provide soft drinks. (Movie breaks are riskier, because they require an hour and a half or two hours and it's harder to find a lighthearted film that everyone enjoys.)
- **Pizza or sub lunches.** People love a free lunch. Order pizzas or submarine sandwiches and arrange for a picnic in a park or other scenic spot near the office.
- **Give awards.** With little warning, announce a "staff meeting" and get everyone together. Then distribute fun prizes to each employee, accompanied by a special recognition. Examples: give a Slinky toy to the "Most Flexible" employee or a baseball bat to the person who's "Most Willing to Go to Bat for This Company." Make sure each employee receives some kind of individual recognition.

MISTAKE PROOFING

Why Wait?

Celebrate often, in small doses, during times of change. Don't wait to hold one big blowout party when a change campaign is over, because you and your staff may never reach a point of tidy, triumphant closure. Even if you do reach the mountaintop, big overhauls usually occur over a year or two. By that time, people may be too burned out to celebrate. Don't wait. Strive to find small successes to celebrate on a regular basis.

A celebration need not involve elaborate planning. Organizational changes can drain everyone's energy, so simply taking the team aside and expressing your heartfelt thanks works wonders. Then let your employees leave early today or arrive late tomorrow.

Commemorate the daily acts of dedication and fortitude that inspire others on the team to bear down and keep plugging away. Rather than dwell on long-term objectives, hail every small win as a worthy accomplishment. If the light at the end of the tunnel is too far off, people will give up looking for it.

Surviving Upheaval at the Top

For unsuspecting employees, management shakeups are like the ultimate electric shock. Managers often feel cast adrift or anxious about their future when there's turnover among their bosses. They may figure the new regime will cut jobs, scale back benefits, or initiate other adverse changes.

They often feel frustrated as well when high-level executives come and go. A supervisor who has built trust and credibility with a well-respected boss may resent having to start all over again cultivating a stranger. Promises or assurances made by the outgoing leader now hang in limbo. If your division president has led you to believe that you're in line for a raise or promotion, but then suddenly gets replaced, you may feel a sense of betrayal along with your other worries.

Making the Worst of a Change

When I worked at an insurance company years ago, we arrived on Monday to learn a beloved vice president had resigned suddenly and a new VP was hired. The incoming VP, Dan, met with us and seemed nice enough. But within hours a group of managers decided to reject him: "He's too young," "He's from a company that doesn't know insurance," "He didn't seem sincere when he spoke with us," "He's in over his head—he'll never make it." Problems spread as some of the managers refused to give Dan the support he needed. Morale swooned. Dan wound up having to terminate some longtime managers, which further eroded trust in him. Although conditions improved in time, the negative reactions of the group of managers caused this change to be far more difficult for all.

Even more serious problems can erupt when the incoming boss or bosses lack the credentials or background that managers deem necessary for the position. When new faces show up in positions of power, managers become critics. They scour any newcomer's work history and education with a sharp eye. They inevitably hear and pass along rumors, such as "He fired everyone in his last job" or "She's known for dissing middle managers." All too often, managers form strong negative opinions about freshly hired executives before their first meeting.

When there's upheaval among your organization's leaders, refrain from snap judgments. Don't criticize every move. Monitor events as they unfold without adding a running commentary. Expect at least some of your colleagues to lash out at the personnel changes or question the rationale of all the shuffling, but resist the urge to chime in too soon. Wait for the dust to settle before you render a verdict.

It's easy to overreact to major changes in your organization's top ranks. When new faces appear out of nowhere to run part or all of your company, you or your coworkers might view the events in extreme terms ("We're goners now! There goes any chance we had to survive!").

In reality, however, a management shakeup can work either for or against you. By watching, waiting, and reserving judgment, you give newcomers a chance and avoid stigmatizing yourself as a cynic or a critic. The best way to weather changes in the executive suite is to act like a team player, at least until you can evaluate the new regime fairly and decide what's best for your career.

Transforming Resistance to Acceptance

"So what's the problem?" I asked a friend who sought my advice about his job running an in-house print shop for a large corporation.

"We've got to clamp down on costs, use the new equipment properly, and stop doing things wastefully the way we've always

---

I'm Your Humble Servant

Great managers show "servant leadership": they view their job **Smart** as supporting and serving their employees. In turbulent times, **Managing** step into your employees' shoes and see problems from their perspective. Tell yourself, "By fixing their problems, I fix mine" and "It's not whether they resist change, it's whether I make it easy for them to change." Show interest in their plight and empathize with their concerns. Only after you've invested time in understanding their views of change can you induce them to see the benefits of replacing the status quo.

---

done them," he said. "Basically, I have to get people to break their habits when they don't want to let go of them."

Like so many workplace problems, this one boiled down to perspective. From my friend's vantage point, the issue was getting his employees to stop resisting change. But the employees' problem was dealing with a pushy taskmaster who wouldn't let them do their jobs the right way.

The manager's solution? Reframe the problem.

Rather than define it as a "workers resist change" issue, I urged my friend to recast it as a communication challenge.

"That's right," I told my friend. "The problem starts with *you* and how you communicate to them."

"Oh, come on," he said, scoffing. "Don't give me that line about how they're innocent and I'm guilty, that I'm really the cause of the problem."

When your employees fight change, the real problem often *does* revolve around you. It's your responsibility to persuade your employees to achieve their goals faster, more safely, and more easily. How? Appeal to their self-interest and guide them to follow your lead. Stop thinking, "They just won't get with the program" or "I've tried everything but they won't listen" and start dangling carrots that entice them to want to change.

To woo employees to buy into change, let them tell you what motivates them and how they think they can best achieve work-related objectives. Skip the lectures about what's at stake and why change must happen. Follow these guidelines:

- **Listen for understanding, not agreement.** Realize that your workers' perception of change may clash with yours. Don't take it personally or adopt an adversarial stance. Listen first, disagree later. Strive to understand their fears, concerns, and ideas about changes. Ask lots of follow-up questions so that you fully appreciate their point of view.
- **Shove aside your problems.** Sure, you're under pressure to get your employees to comply with changes and keep them all focused on results. But if you're too insistent on getting what *you* want, you'll alienate the very people you need most on your side—your employees. Concentrate on their priorities, not yours. Only after you fully understand their position should you begin to consider how your needs overlap with theirs.
- **Forge an alliance.** After you listen and learn, propose ways for employees to get what they want by accepting organizational change. Use phrases such as "Here's how you can achieve that...." or "You can get what you're looking for by...." Keep yourself and your needs out of it!

CAUTION!

Treat Issues, Not Personalities

Face it: you may not like an employee who resists change. You're already stressed by all the recent turmoil in your company and now you've got to deal with angry, anxious workers who put up a fight. Vent in private. When you're on the job, concentrate on solving the problem with open, intensive communication. Don't focus on the person. Acknowledging your personal dislikes—whether to yourself or to others—will only force you to work harder to listen and gain understanding.

Above all, give employees the benefit of the doubt when they raise objections to change campaigns. Hear them out. Dignify their opinions by saying, "I see your point" or "That's a possibility." By showing that you're willing to admit that their points are at least somewhat valid, you can reduce their resistance and promote mutual trust.

Manager's Checklist for Chapter 9

❏ Build employees' confidence as change sets in. Praise them for being flexible and open. Don't assume they'll resist any shifts in the status quo.

❏ If an employee appears stressed, dig for the underlying cause. Don't assume that it's change alone that's to blame.

❏ Communicate about change in increments. Present each phase of a reorganization as a small, bite-size chunk that's easier for employees to swallow.

❏ Apply the "incremental yes" technique by persuading staffers to make small sacrifices. From that point, ask them to gradually accept bigger inconveniences.

❏ Avoid making too many predictions. Level with people about what you know for sure—and admit what you don't know.

❏ Hold small, frequent celebrations to boost morale. That's better than waiting to throw a giant party.

❏ When there's upheaval among your organization's leaders, withhold snap judgments and criticisms. Let the dust settle first.

❏ When employees resist change, listen to their concerns. Then lead them to accept change by showing them how it's in their best interests.

Motivating Employees Against All Odds

It's easy to motivate wildly enthusiastic employees—the ones who wake up every morning, race to the office, and arrive with the energy and dedication to excel. Get out of their way and you'll look like a genius.

Yet these driven, delightful self-starters are a dying breed in these uncertain times. Today's workers fret about everything from economic downturns—and the layoffs that often accompany them—to care-giving responsibilities (for their children or parents) to getting stuck in boring, dead-end jobs. Most of these distracted or disenchanted individuals don't feel deep loyalty to any employer and may refuse to make sacrifices when the organization hits a rough patch.

That leaves you as manager attempting to motivate people who may lack your commitment and your willingness to withstand hardship for the greater good. To make matters worse, many bosses expect employees to push harder in a high-pressure, fast-turnaround environment. They need to work well in teams, learn and develop new skills, adapt to constant changes, take more risks and responsibility for results, and exhibit creativity and initiative.

That's a lot to ask.

Under such adverse conditions, it's no wonder that many managers struggle to motivate employees. There's a temptation to surrender, to adopt a laissez-faire attitude and forgo

> ### Money Talks
>
> Ian, a sales manager at a home inspection firm, wanted his employees to treat customers better after he received a rash of complaints about their surly attitudes. His solution? He promised to pay them a cash bonus for every three letters that customers sent in praise of their behavior. That simple strategy raised his employees' commitment to service to a higher level.

the rah-rah cheerleading. These managers may sit back and wait for a handful of self-starters to rise to the top while the rest fall by the wayside.

At the other extreme, you might take an active role in motivating your troops. You try everything from dangling carrots to poking them with sticks. You can stay up at night devising rules for your next big contest or incentive program or you announce higher standards and insist that all employees "elevate their game" and make a greater contribution.

If you're going to experiment with motivational strategies, send the right message. Make it easy for everyone to understand how their level of effort will pay off with certain rewards and recognition.

> ### Got Alignment?
>
> You get what you reward. Choose the wrong things to reward and you'll compound your problems. If you want your staffers to answer phones promptly (say, within two rings), they may comply but sound harried or rude to callers. Reward activity and you can wind up with workers rushing around doing lots of pointless busy work; reward results and you can motivate with more precision.

Stepping Back from the Fray

When employees present a problem to you, don't rush to provide solutions. Ask what they think first. If you lecture them or reel off a list of demands, you're going to kill their desire to draw their own conclusions.

Managers often assume they must have answers to all their employees' questions. They may also figure it's their job to give the right answer, right away. You may be thinking, "Well, it saves time and clarifies things if I tell employees what they need to know to solve problems and answer their questions head on." You're right—in part.

There's just one catch: employees who get quick, easy answers will not grow as a result. Whenever there's a problem, they'll come to you for snappy solutions without grappling with problems on their own.

For a smarter motivational tactic, learn to ask questions like Socrates, the Greek philosopher. "If you know what to ask, you can basically get the answer," said James Parker, CEO of Southwest Airlines, in *Investor's Business Daily* (Nov. 12, 2001, p. 1). That means choosing questions that lead people to solve problems. Empower your employees to find out for themselves what they're after and you'll motivate them in all kinds of ways.

Here are examples of smart questions you can ask when employees battle with a problem:

- "How does this compare with what's happened in the past? What worked or did not work at that time?"
- "If you could wave a magic wand, how would you solve this? To what extent is that solution realistic?"
- "Would you prefer that someone else step in and solve this or would you like to see this through to a conclusion? Why?"
- "If I weren't around, what would you do?" (alternate version: "If you had my job, what would you do?")

When your employees answer one of these questions, follow up with another question. Keep the inquiries coming! You'll motivate employees more effectively by prodding them to analyze the situation from all sides.

Employees may need an extra push if they're grappling with

Apply the Three-Question Rule

Motivate your employees to overcome obstacles and solve problems by withholding your advice or directions until you've asked three questions first. Start with a broad inquiry, such as "What have you tried so far?" or one of the questions listed above. Then ask a specific follow-up based on their answer, such as "What did you discover when you tried that?" Finally, ask what other factors or variables might influence the situation, such as "Is there anything else that can affect the outcome?" This trio of questions enables employees to assess a problem thoroughly while helping you understand what's at stake and how you can guide them toward a solution.

process management. You may know instantly how to unclog a bottleneck in an assembly line or streamline purchasing procedures. Although it's easier to tell your employees what to do and how to do it, it will cause them to run to you whenever they're frustrated. It will also convey the message that you don't trust them to be able to deal with the problems. That's hardly an empowering motivational technique.

Winning Over Lower-Level Workers

Among the toughest management challenges for problem-plagued supervisors is preventing their staff from giving up or turning into cynics or naysayers. Entry level employees are especially prone to burn out in a crisis. They may buckle when subjected to a pressurized work environment with high-strung managers racing around trying to put out fires.

You may love what you do and think nothing of working 12-hour days. But your employees may not all share your enthusiasm. Take these steps to motivate them.

1. Practice proper delegation. If you're like most managers, you already know you should delegate more. But that doesn't mean dumping only the most onerous jobs onto your employees. It's smarter to dole out stimulating, coveted assignments along with a smattering of lower-profile tasks. Don't unintentionally punish top performers by giving them a steady stream of difficult, unglamorous, or backbreaking jobs.

2. Give them what they want. One of the easiest ways to motivate entry-level employees is to satisfy their reasonable requests. When they ask for new equipment or resources—and they show why it's a cost-effective investment—follow through on their behalf. When they want to leave an hour or two early for a valid reason, agree without demanding concessions or making them feel guilty. The key is to add, "I'm doing this for you because you deserve it" or "You make a good case for me to do that for you, so it's easy to say yes." This shows you're not a pushover *and* rewards their hard work and valuable contribution.

3. Focus on the positive. Dispense praise generously. Take every opportunity to tell employees what you admire about their performance, attitude, and behavior. But don't stop there. When chatting with your staff, marvel at your customers for their loyalty during tough times. Express respect for a peer who runs another department. Compliment a computer consultant for diagnosing a problem quickly and recommending sensible steps to fix it. Your employees will follow your lead and look for what's right, not what's wrong. And they'll be more enthusiastic when they know they work for someone who focuses on the positive.

If your employees seem discontented, *you* might be the problem. No matter how much bad luck swirls around you, keep cool and model the kind of behavior you want your staffers to emulate. Stay positive. Admire what's right rather

Here's What I Think...

James supervised a group of clerical assistants at an insurance firm. After years of cutbacks at his company, he grew jaded and negative. He'd lash out in all directions, lambasting his bosses, peers, and employees. One day, he told me he read an article in *The New York Times* about Brooke Astor, a 99-year-old Manhattan socialite and philanthropist. She said, "If you don't like someone, you don't have to say anything. You don't have to say something about everyone." He took her comment to heart and he gradually began to share positive opinions—or keep quiet.

than harping on defects, mishaps, and defeats. Set a great example that will motivate them to follow your lead.

Cheering from a Distance

More than 25 million Americans telecommute, according to the International Telework Association & Council. There are also thousands of field employees who work in a different site from their manager, such as client support specialists who are stationed closer to customers.

When you supervise off-site employees, you must motivate them from afar. That's a tall order. Many bosses struggle to motivate employees who work right outside their office. Just imagine the difficulty of stirring up passion in people hundreds of miles away.

Motivating always requires strong communication skills. When you're working with employees at a distance, it's especially important that you listen well on the phone and write clear e-mails. You develop a "phone personality" and an "e-mail personality" when you supervise from afar. Employees learn to read your moods by your tone of voice or the choice of words in your memos.

In phone conversations with employees, speak with energy and enthusiasm. Use vocal inflection to emphasize action words ("Let's *run* with that idea," "Now it's time to *boost* our results," "We'll *solve* each of these problems"). Sound like you enjoy talking with your employees, not like it's a chore or an obligation. You don't need to exchange pleasantries every time; it's more important that you acknowledge their input and follow up when they ask questions or drop hints about what they want from you.

Are you besieged by problems? Keep them to yourself. Don't sigh into the phone or curse under your breath. Employees pick up on your cues. Because they can't see you in your lighter moments, their only basis for judging your mood is how you sound during phone conversations. Your feelings of gloom, disgust, or disapproval might spread like wildfire if your field workforce detects negative emotions from your tone.

The same goes when you write. Employees will read between the lines. Are you impatient? Annoyed? Skeptical? Fearful? When workers can't see you every day, they lack access to the full range of signals that indicate what you think and feel. That magnifies the importance of every message you write to them, whether it's a scribbled fax, a formal memo, or a rushed e-mail.

To make matters worse, some managers adopt a stiff formality when they express themselves in writing. They may lace their sentences with extraneous phrases such as "Please be advised that" or "As per our conversation of March 5...." A teleworker recently told me, "Whenever I get an e-mail from my boss, it sounds as if he's firing me even when he's just asking for something minor. He writes like a lawyer, even though he never talks that way."

Write the Right Way

Follow the four A's of good business writing to motivate off-site employees:

1. **Attention grabber.** Convey urgency or timeliness in the first line. This way, readers will know you're serious. *Examples:* "We're entering the three most critical weeks of the year" or "Terrific changes are in store."
2. **Acknowledge negatives.** Anticipate and disarm readers who might resist your message. By conveying empathy, you ally yourself with them. *Examples:* "I realize this hardly makes things easier for you" or "This doesn't solve everything."
3. **Assert positives.** Here's where you shift gears and attempt to motivate. Offset the negatives with positives, perhaps by contrasting short-term risks with long-term rewards or reframing defeats as victories. *Examples:* "In the long run, this bodes well for us" or "This is actually a blessing in disguise."
4. **Appreciate what's right.** End on an upbeat note. Thank the employee for cooperating. Praise new ideas or recognize excellent effort. *Examples:* "You continue to play a key role in helping us through this" or "Thank you in advance for doing a great job on this."

A friendly reminder such as "Don't forget to clean the filter before you leave" can seem like a scolding when it's put into print. And if you start too many sentences with commandments ("Stop sending in so many activity reports," "Finish your proposals first," "Spend less time dealing with salespeople," "Don't negotiate with suppliers"), you risk coming across as too bossy.

Salvaging Post-Layoff Morale

Motivating employees in the aftermath of layoffs may seem like an exercise in futility. Seeing empty desks where their colleagues once worked can turn your remaining employees into guilty, grieving, or bitter survivors. Rather than feel relief that they still have a job, they may turn against you and your organization for allowing layoffs.

Traditional motivational techniques rarely work with post-layoff employees. They don't respond well to praise because they're too anxious or upset to treat it seriously. They may not care if you assign them more exciting jobs because they're sapped of enthusiasm. Dangling incentives, such as cash bonuses and gift certificates, for individuals who attain ambitious production goals can't hurt. But shell-shocked employees may simply ignore the carrots and put in the minimum work effort. Throwing parties or hosting other celebrations may backfire as well.

"I couldn't believe that after we let 10 great people go with little notice and no severance, management was giving us all these free lunches and toasting our wonderful future," an auditor at an accounting firm told me. "None of us felt right being happy at that time. And I was really offended by the lip service paid to the people who were shoved out the door. Thanking them 'for their fine service' adds insult to injury after you treat them so poorly."

So if the classic motivational moves are off limits, what can you do to keep your employees from turning against you after layoffs? *Give them a sense of control over their jobs.*

Help employees understand the link between their contribution and the organization's overall profit and loss. Empower them to work smarter by teaching them how to measure the same key ratios you and your bosses use to evaluate the business. Examples vary by industry, but typically include output measures for each employee such as the following:

- Files closed or completed
- Phone calls answered
- Customers helped
- Orders processed

Beware of adopting a meet-your-quota-or-else approach. This will embitter employees, not motivate them. Instead, explain why output drives the business and how the efforts and work habits of each individual directly affect the bottom line.

If you focus on sales or revenue generated per employee, educate your employees on what they can do to boost sales. Provide training, resources, and other tools so they're equipped to succeed. If there's no budget for investing in your people, alert them to resources they can tap on their own if they want to protect themselves against layoffs.

At the same time, launch an aggressive campaign to solicit ideas and recommendations from them. If you show that you treat their input seriously and act on it, then you motivate

Post "Idea Ground Rules"

Smart Managing To spur employees to submit ideas and recommend ways for the organization to regain momentum after layoffs, spread the word by setting ground rules that encourage workers to participate. For example, specify that there are three guiding principles:
1. Everything can be improved.
2. Everyone in every job is capable of contributing ideas to improve.
3. Every idea will be evaluated and everyone will get a quick reply.

Post these principles on a central bulletin board. Distribute flyers, paycheck stuffers, and other reminders to reinforce this idea-generating campaign.

them to think like CEOs. Engage them in the business more deeply and they'll feel a new sense of control.

Realize that survivors need to vent after layoffs occur. Let employees express their fears and concerns freely. Don't shun them if they complain. Listen sympathetically and offer encouragement and support. This type of motivation is a quieter and more dignified approach that shows people you understand what they're going through.

Peeling Away Perks

Motivating people after layoffs is hard enough. But many organizations suffering from an economic downturn must scale back perks for the remaining workers. That compounds the problem of preserving morale.

If bad times force you to reassess your employee benefits, try to reduce rather than eliminate perks. If you offer free lunch to employees every Friday, for instance, maintain the program but limit it to once a month.

Better yet, ask workers to share the cost rather than make them feel powerless. By soliciting workers' feedback on which perks they prize the most, you can incorporate their preferences into your decisions.

Earlier in this chapter, we discussed ways to motivate lower-level workers. If you must cut benefits, don't target these folks. Spread the pain among all levels. This motivates everyone to stay the course.

> **Plug Leaks, Stop Rumors** **CAUTION!**
>
> If you've experienced layoffs, you surely appreciate the value of controlling the grapevine. When rumors fly of impending job cuts, productivity grinds to a halt. The same goes when you're weighing a cut in employee benefits. Prevent leaks. Rather than drop hints in committee meetings or make occasional offhand comments, wait to spill the news to everyone at once. Explain the need for reductions and invite feedback from your employees.

Battling a More Powerful Rival

The 2002 Super Bowl featured the heavily favored defending champions, the St. Louis Rams, losing in the last minute to the upstart New England Patriots. Many sports commentators called it one of the most thrilling championship football games ever.

People love to root for the underdog. Fans cheered when the team of superstars was dethroned by a gritty team led by a rookie quarterback and a bunch of relative unknowns.

There's a lesson here for managers struggling to motivate employees against a mightier, richer, or bigger competitor. Take pride in playing the "spoiler." Turn the fact that your organization's not as powerful into an advantage by emphasizing your team's versatility, flexibility, and responsiveness to abrupt shifts in the marketplace. Use your underdog status to rally employees to work together. They'll lift each other to new heights and dig deep within themselves to deliver exceptional performance if they're driven by a collective will to win—a challenge to conquer seemingly insurmountable odds.

Us Against the World

Smart underdogs embrace their role. When Komatsu, a manufacturer of construction parts and equipment, rallied its workforce to trounce its larger competitor, Caterpillar, it adopted the slogan "Encircle Caterpillar!" When Canon, a maker of photocopy machines, set out to expand its market share against the bigger Xerox, its rallying cry became "Beat Xerox!" Both companies succeeded by galvanizing their workers to pull together to fight a mighty rival.

Expect employees to express doubts and question whether you and the top brass can lead your organization to trounce a formidable rival. You'll need to keep lighting a spark under them so they don't lapse into hopelessness or cynicism. How? Wear your "game face" in front of employees to show you're determined to achieve victory. Sulk in private, if you must. Recognize small wins and reward them. Create a rallying cry that reminds everyone of your mission.

If your competitor gains the upper hand and your organization's prospects look grim, remain hopeful. Your employees will follow your lead, so focus on what's right and see the silver lining in every setback. As the head of a fast-growing company told me, "You need to be optimistic to the point of being insane." Say a rival firm introduces a product that will take a bite out of your market share or initiates costly litigation to bleed your cash reserves. Maintain a positive attitude by telling your workers, "We *will* be successful" or "Through all this, we're going to survive and prosper." Acknowledge the challenges ahead, but end by appealing to everyone's strength, perseverance, and dedication.

Giving Feedback That Pays Off

When managers tell me they're struggling to motivate their staff, that they've "tried everything" but they're unable to lift their team's performance, I ask one simple question: *What's your Praise/Criticism Ratio?*

This ratio of positive feedback to negative feedback largely determines whether you're a motivator or a taskmaster. By doling out praise generously and limiting your criticism to specific, descriptive, performance-related observations, you drive your employees to excel while bolstering their self-worth.

Positive input should outweigh negative feedback. Almost all managers know this, yet few actually keep the praise flowing freely. For many of us, the problem starts when we're youngsters at school where we are criticized more often than we are praised. Sadly, it isn't that different in many workplaces.

Tell people what they do well and they're more likely to repeat it. Tell people what they don't know or how they messed up and they're more apt to stew in resentment. What you perceive as your hard-charging, tell-it-like-it-is management style can come across as bullying to employees who already doubt their ability and need supportive guidance to improve.

Performance reviews can serve as an ideal motivational tool—or squash whatever traces of enthusiasm a worker has left. It depends on how you communicate during these one-on-one sessions with your employees. Use the PAID method to make sure your input leaves a lasting positive impression:

Past. Begin by discussing how the employee has improved in the past few months. Refer to the last performance review and any interim meetings you've had since then. *Example*: "When we last spoke about your filing, I was concerned about your lack of accuracy. Well, it's clear to me that you've improved tremendously in that regard."

Admire. Convey sincere admiration for some aspect of the employee's performance. Speak with energy, radiate excitement, and use your body language to show that you're genuinely delighted for the individual's success (say, by smiling and flashing the thumbs-up sign). *Example*: "Your willingness to test new approaches and measure which one works best sets an example for all of us. I really like what you've done and how you've conducted yourself."

Improve. Never follow praise with a "but." Instead, pause after you express your admiration and segue into laying out how the employee can improve. Maintain your positive tone; don't turn grim, clear your throat, or sound as if you're sad or upset having to shift from praise to criticism. Use phrases such as "Here's where you need to improve..." or "One area of your performance that we should discuss is...." *Example*: "Here's where you could stand to improve: your speed. Now more than ever, we all need to operate efficiently. I'd like you to raise your efficiency so that you get more done in less time."

Develop a plan. End on a high note by working with the employee on a performance plan, a map to improve that consists of manageable, measurable stages. *Example*: "Let's develop a plan together on how you can work faster without sacrificing the excellent results you've been able to achieve."

The easiest way to prevent morale problems is to dish out praise in generous portions. Monitor your Praise/Criticism Ratio and you cannot help but lift employees' spirits *and* performance. Recognize what people do right, let them know, and express your admiration. Then repeat.

Miss the Start, Miss the End

When reviewing an employee's performance, consider *all* the evidence. Don't neglect the "excluded middle." The initial information we get about someone influences us strongly, along with the most recent information. So if you harp on what you first observed the employee doing six months or a year ago—and you jump to what you just noticed in the days before the performance appraisal—you risk overlooking the individual's work during all the months in between.

Manager's Checklist for Chapter 10

❏ When employees come to you with a problem, don't provide solutions. Ask questions instead so they think for themselves.

❏ When entry-level workers make reasonable requests, such as asking for low-cost tools to help them do their jobs, say yes without a fuss. Your quick responsiveness will motivate them.

❏ Keep your problems to yourself when you're talking to off-site employees. Don't sigh into the phone or curse under your breath. Employees pick up on your cues.

❏ Write memos to employees in a conversational style. Avoid stringing together lots of "do this, do that" orders or you risk coming across as bossy.

❏ After layoffs, allow survivors to express their fears and concerns freely. Listen sympathetically, offer support, and solicit their ideas.

❏ To reduce rumors, communicate organizational news to everyone at once. That's better than dropping hints or leaking information to a few employees beforehand.

❏ Track your ratio of praise to criticism so that you motivate employees by recognizing their accomplishments.

Mapping a Problem-Prevention Plan

G ene, a versatile VP of a health maintenance organization, agreed to expand his duties and run the claims department after the CEO said, "We need someone like you to go into claims and clean it up before it becomes unmanageable."

At the time, the claims department had developed a reputation as an inefficient operation that ground out mediocre results year after year. It wasn't mired in problems as much as hampered by low expectations, antiquated systems, and an apathetic staff.

From his first day in claims, Gene knew he needed to change the mindset of the employees from problem acceptance to problem prevention. He told them, "Our mission is simple. We need to sort out what we do right and what we do wrong. Then we need to figure out how to do more of what's right and stop doing what's wrong."

Problem prevention starts with great communication. By leveling with employees about what must happen for them to produce better outcomes—and responding to their ideas and requests for resources—you show that you're going to fight problems head on and stop them.

Gene spent his first few weeks as head of the claims department meeting privately with key individuals in the unit. He asked each of them three questions:

- *What do you see as the biggest problems facing this department?*
- *What do you think* I *can do to prevent those problems?*
- *What do you think* you *can do to prevent those problems?*

After holding dozens of these one-on-one discussions, Gene not only established rapport with the people he'd need to enlist in his problem-prevention campaign, but also learned what issues most plagued his employees.

But Gene didn't stop there. He also met with about 10 customers—external and internal—to ask similar questions. (When interviewing policyholders—the HMO's external customers—he modified his third question as "What do you think *our employees* can do to prevent those problems?")

Finally, Gene upgraded his data gathering by examining the claims department's productivity numbers. He knew that payroll costs were soaring while the unit's output remained sluggish, so he devised a way to measure productivity per employee based on the number of claims settled within set timeframes. The numbers enabled him to make clear performance comparisons among employees and alerted Gene of personnel issues that needed attention.

Gene made substantial headway in his first few months on the job. By listening to his staff and diagnosing weaknesses in the operation, he took steps to bolster productivity and morale before serious problems could arise.

To safely travel the bumpy road that leads to the executive suite, follow Gene's lead. Prevent problems. Engage in plenty of researching, observing, and questioning. Identify what's wrong now and what's likely to go wrong if nothing's done to stop it. Then take action, measure the results, and rally the team to join you on your problem-prevention crusade.

Selecting "Solution Czars"

As a manager, you're in charge of preventing problems, whether you realize it or not. But you need not act alone. Deputize a group of key employees as "solution czars" to help you spot problems early and enact prompt, workable solutions.

In choosing your solution czars, look for high-energy, independent thinkers who bring intelligence and commitment to the job. Assemble a team of about five to 10 czars from all levels, including support staff, technicians, administrators, and first-line supervisors. Help them clear time from their schedules so they can treat problem prevention as a "single-focus activity" for a few hours a week. You may need to reassign other employees to fill in for your czars when they're engaged in problem-prevention activities. Otherwise, they may feel overburdened and struggle to concentrate when pulled away from their regular jobs.

Gather your solution czars every two weeks for a team meeting. Devote the first few minutes to listing current problems and potential problems. Then brainstorm to identify solutions. Keep the focus on positive steps individuals can take, from adopting new procedures to following old ones more closely. If a czar requests money or other resources to implement some promising ideas, work together on a cost-benefit analysis to evaluate the probable payoff. Invest only in solutions for which a czar agrees to be held accountable for results.

Keep your team firmly rooted in reality. Some solution czars get carried away by their ideas, especially if this is their first

> **Key Term** **Role strain** Conflict within a role, caused by dueling priorities. When you ask employees to commit a chunk of time to an additional activity that's above and beyond their normal duties (such as joining a team), they may suffer role strain. They may need your help managing their time so they don't overextend themselves or burn out. Role strain and vague job descriptions go hand in hand: If people don't know what they're supposed to do, they can keep taking on projects to the point where they can't finish anything they start.

opportunity to join a high-profile group devoted to fixing what's broken in the workplace. A manager in a Nevada mining company told me that one of his solution czars had "big arms." When I asked what that meant, he replied, "It's slang in our business for stretching, for promoting the upside of your idea so much that your arms get bigger and bigger as you talk about it."

Encourage your czars to talk among themselves so you can sit back and listen. Your role at problem-prevention meetings is to focus everyone on what matters most. They shouldn't look for your approval or guidance every step of the way. The more they bounce off each other by exchanging ideas and sharing information, the more likely you'll collect their best input and come away with more susbtantive, powerful solutions.

Charles Schwab's Secret

In 1904, Ivy Lee, a prominent management consultant and a pioneer among "efficiency experts," advised managers at Bethlehem Steel on how to solve production problems. One day, Lee reportedly paid an unscheduled visit to Bethlehem Steel's president, Charles Schwab. Lee promised to give Schwab an idea to help him prevent problems by organizing his time more effectively.

"Since I've dropped in on you today, I don't expect you to pay me," Lee said. "Just use the idea and see what you think. If it pays off, share it with your staff. And if you feel the idea's worthwhile and you want to pay me later for it, I'll accept whatever you decide it's worth."

Schwab accepted these terms and asked for the idea.

"At the start of each day, list in ranked order the six most important things you have to do," Lee explained. "Then begin with No. 1, and continue to work until you've finished it. When you're done with the first task, reevaluate the other five items to make sure nothing's changed your ranking. Then go to No. 2. When it's done, reevaluate, then work on No. 3."

Lee assured Schwab that, even if by day's end all six items were not completed, progress had still occurred. "You wouldn't

Rank the Right Way

Smart Managing When you rank your top six to-do items at the beginning of the day, think in terms of which tasks will prevent or lessen problems that might otherwise undermine your ability to make a bottom-line impact on your organization. As you weigh the ranking of each item on your list, ask yourself, "If I ignore this, what problems will result? What are the costs of inaction?" The greater the cost of doing nothing, the higher you should prioritize the task.

have finished all six things using any other method, either. And at least you did the most important things. And even if you didn't even complete the No. 1 task, you were still working on the most important thing you had to do."

Schwab liked what he heard. A few months later, after successfully applying the idea, he mailed Lee a check for $25,000—a huge sum at the time. He told Lee it was "the most important idea I've received all year," according to *How to Make the Most of Your Workday* by Peg Pickering (Franklin Lakes, NJ: Career Press, 2001, pp. 98-99).

Like Charles Schwab, you need a system to tackle your top-priority projects. Minor mishaps can spiral out of control when managers fail to address them early on. If you confront problems in sequence, starting with the most pressing, you prevent them from mushrooming into major disasters.

The most organized managers take a proactive approach to solving problems. They don't wait for something bad to get worse; instead, they acknowledge that something's bad and take immediate steps to correct it.

Talking a Good Game

In the aftermath of the 2001 terrorist attacks on New York's World Trade Center, a Manhattan investment bank had to relocate its offices from Ground Zero to New Jersey. The managing director of the bank turned uncharacteristically quiet in the following months. Rather than discuss the traumatic experience with his staff, he brooded and worked behind closed doors. By early 2002, he lost much of his power to lead because he had refused

> **Silo mentality** A narrow perspective in which employees and managers think first (or only) in terms of their own department, not in connection with other departments or within the context of the whole organization. When managers hunker down in their offices (i.e., silos) and isolate themselves from others, they tend to adopt a fragmented, problem-producing mindset. They ignore the interrelationships among people, abandon team efforts, and wait for further crises in a defensive and often panicky frame of mind. Exhibiting a silo mentality, as opposed to taking bold steps to prevent problems, almost guarantees that you'll face more frequent and severe setbacks in the future.

to communicate with his team about the tragedy they all lived through. As I write this, he's facing mounting personnel problems.

Had this executive shared his feelings with his employees—and listened to their concerns and anxieties—he could have created a more supportive work environment. The adjustment would still be hard and slow, of course, but with open communication at least all of the employees could pull together and forge emotional bonds to strengthen their resolve to persevere.

While most of us won't suffer through such a horrific experience, this sad story reminds us that it's generally wise to talk out our concerns with colleagues. Discussing your fears and anxieties with others won't necessarily prevent bad outcomes, but it will raise awareness so that everyone attempts to do their part to enact a solution.

Talking about potential problems with trusted coworkers and employees can help prevent them. But that's not enough. You also need to speak positive, proactive language. Use fair, descriptive terms when referring to others. Withhold harsh judgments or dismissive labels. If you call workers "lazy bums" or declare them "brain dead," for example, you may laugh and think you're poking harmless fun at them. In reality, however, you'll cause morale problems. Employees will "live down" to your expectations. They will hear how you refer to them and, rather than laugh along, they may conclude there's no reason to change your mind.

Choose words such as "hard-working," "dedicated," and "inspiring" to describe the members of your team and they'll start demonstrating those qualities. If you want to lead staffers to stamp out problems, say, "We will overcome this!" or "Together we can do this!" Your words as manager carry more power than you may realize. Convey optimism and faith in the positive facets of their personalities and skills and they can become your allies in preventing problems.

Planning to Fail

Manage long enough and you'll fail—big time. Your error may result in the loss of a major account for your company. Your miscommunication with a star employee may drive that person to quit. Your decision to deploy your organization's resources in a high-risk, high-reward mission may bring no reward—but lots of grief.

Problem prevention and contingency planning go hand in hand. By weighing the full range of consequences of your actions, you can eliminate problems or at least contain their damage.

Preventing Problem Presentations

Contingency planning works especially well if you want to prevent problems related to public speaking and presentations. I tell nervous presenters to decide in advance how they'll react to an assortment of dreaded outcomes, such as a heckler

TRICKS OF THE TRADE

Conquer Worst-Case Blues

Before you launch a project or take a calculated risk, ask a mentor or trusted peer, "What's the worst that can happen?" Then add your own worst-case scenario to the mix. Now that you have a thorough sense of the dangers, ask, "OK, then what?" Work with your advisor on how you would rebound in the event that everything fell apart. Through this exercise, you can draft emergency plans and take precautionary steps now to mitigate damage later. By imagining you're living through your worst managerial nightmare, you can plot your response in a calm, calculated manner.

in the audience, a technological breakdown (say, an Internet freeze-up in the middle of a Web-based computer demonstration), or an embarrassingly small turnout for their speech.

The best way to prevent problems is to plan carefully; the less you leave to chance, the more easily you can cope with whatever surprises pop up. Here's an example. If you're going to show slides, your first step in preparing a successful presentation should involve breaking your content into three sections. Then assign each slide to one of your three sections. How? Take a blank sheet of paper, create three columns with the headings "Act I," "Act II," and "Act III" and note where each slide belongs. This exercise will help you strike slides from your presentation that don't correspond to your three-prong structure.

Poor presenters without a well-crafted plan might figure, "I was asked to speak for 30 minutes, so I better calculate how many slides to squeeze into that time." They may wind up with a choppy, slide-heavy presentation that's impossible for the audience to follow.

Right Person, Right Job

By devising a strategy for each worst case, you gain immeasurable confidence. You'll approach the task with the peace of mind of knowing that you won't allow any mishaps to derail your progress.

Contingency planning also pays off when you manage staff. As much as you try to put the right people into the right jobs, there's always the chance of a mismatch. This tends to happen when a manager promotes employees into positions for which they lack the skills or training to succeed. By devising a Plan B in case the worker fails in the new post (such as breaking one job into two or outsourcing a hard-to-fill role), a manager need not watch events unfold helplessly.

Aside from planning for the worst case, a wise manager might build in extra time for a freshly promoted employee to adjust to the new job. Take the case of Rick, a technician who was promoted to supervise six people. He knew his new role far exceeded what he'd been trained to do. But his company was undergoing major changes and people at all levels found themselves in new jobs that they lacked the experience to handle.

"At the time, no one at the top really had the luxury of thinking 'Is this the right person for the job?'" Rick recalls. "It boiled down to plugging holes quickly so changes could proceed."

Sure enough, Rick struggled at first as a supervisor. But his boss took him aside and said, "You're going to sink before we swim. Maybe it'll feel like you're in too deep. I know it'll take you a while to feel comfortable. All I ask is that you adjust for mistakes and learn on the job."

With that encouragement, Rick persevered. He didn't panic. He understood he was in over his head, but that didn't faze him because he knew his boss was supportive.

Skirting Three Traps

Managers who face constant problems aren't merely unlucky. In most cases, they're largely responsible for their plight.

You'll be a magnet for mishaps if your communication skills are sloppy. Talking too much, too loudly, or too harshly can drive a wedge into your relationships with peers and employees.

> **Key Term**
>
> **Impulsiveness** Here are the four most important words to help you prevent interpersonal problems: *Think before you speak.* Rather than blurt out whatever pops into your head, consider the repercussions of your remarks. Before you say something off the cuff, imagine it's five minutes later. What direction has the conversation taken? Are both parties positively engaged? What you say now sets the stage for what follows, so make sure your comments foster goodwill and help you move toward your goal.

Protect yourself from self-sabotage by fighting off these three communication traps.

Prevent problems by not interrupting speakers in the middle of a sentence, especially if you say something that has no bearing on what they're talking about. Wait for the person to wrap up—and then wait a bit more. By pausing an extra moment before you respond, you signal to others that you're not rushing to impose your words.

Faulty reasoning. In my former job as a manager at an insurance company, I'd interview lots of job candidates to fill supervisory positions. My favorite question: *We're big on critical thinking here. How do you define "critical thinking" and can you give an example of how you've used it in your current job?*

> ## Act Now, If You Must
>
> **CAUTION!**
>
> Harried managers may mistake impulsiveness for decisiveness. They figure they need to make snap decisions or assess and judge a situation instantly, so they rush around all day barking orders. It's fine to show decisiveness if you're under the gun and you have enough facts to draw at least a somewhat intelligent conclusion. But you'll know you're too impulsive if you say or do whatever you want without weighing the implications and consequences.

Once you develop sound reasoning and incorporate it into your work habits, you can avoid dozens of problems that afflict sloppier thinkers. You'll acquire tools and knowledge to help you understand what drives others to say or do things—and that it turn can give you an advantage in guiding them to make smart moves.

Wise thinking takes effort. Many managers shift into auto pilot when they communicate, rendering judgments and jumping to conclusions. Soon enough, they find out too late that their perceptions and conclusions were wrong.

To sharpen your reasoning, you need to exert control over your thinking rather than let it happen automatically. Ask yourself these questions before you start an important and potentially problem-filled conversation:

- What do I need to know or learn from this person?
- What questions must I ask? (Write a list so you don't forget!)
- What assumptions do I bring to the conversation?
- How can I test the accuracy of what I hear?

Know Your Biases

Managers who are blinded by their biases tend to fall into the same reasoning traps over and over. To sweep away your prejudices so that you don't repeatedly misdiagnose problems, state both sides of an issue with equal conviction. Give "on the one hand/on the other hand" summaries as you prepare to meet with someone to resolve a dilemma. Or complete the sentence, "The way they see the situation...." Empathy enables you to appreciate other perspectives, which in turn sharpens your reasoning ability.

Approval dependence. If you chronically seek approval from others, you'll tell them what they want to hear rather than what they need to know. And that's a prime breeding ground for problems.

Smart managers steer clear of conflicts by being fair and sensitive. They focus less on *being liked* than on *building trust*. Ask them what drives their communication with employees and they'll say, "I want to establish mutual respect" rather than "I want us to be friends."

It's futile to hope that your staff will approve of all your actions and decisions. They won't. Your best intentions will backfire on occasion. As long as you direct everyone's attention to shared goals and you communicate forthrightly about how to achieve them, then you increase accountability and set aside your need for approval.

Sprinting to the Finish Line

A frazzled manager of a real estate office grabbed me by the shoulders and said, "I wish there was a button on my keyboard I could press to delete all my problems!"

There's no magic button, but that doesn't mean you're at the mercy of cruel circumstance. From everything you've learned in this book, it should be clear by now that you can not only address problems in their earliest stages, but also prevent them much of the time. It depends on your ability to think ahead, step into others' shoes, and speak and listen well.

Above all, you need a system or procedure to follow as soon as you detect something's awry. If you improvise, you may miss opportunities to mitigate problems before they intensify. While every situation merits a different response, here's a template to use as a starting point to prevent problems from growing:

- **Explain** the situation completely to a mentor or advisor. Present all the facts and the relevant background.
- **Identify** three options on what you can do next. "Do nothing" may count as one. The others can be as broad or specific as you wish.
- **Choose** the best action plan. Collect input from your coach. Conduct additional research as necessary so that you amass all the information you need. Then commit to a course of action that will either stamp out the problem in its tracks or mitigate its damage.

Problems involving both people and processes often stem from benign neglect. Managers are too busy to think proactively. Employees are under pressure to put out fires and follow directions. Seeds of conflict spread, sprout up quickly, and soon envelop the workplace.

Enlightened managers are less prone to face severe

Trackers and Deputies

You cannot prevent problems in a vacuum; you need your employees' help. The key is knowing whom to turn to in a crunch. Search for at least a few workers who qualify as trackers and deputies.

Trackers investigate what you need to know to address problems. Like detectives, they snoop for clues about what's causing, say, a production bottleneck or a dip in morale. They're keen observers, dogged answer-seekers, and curious students of human nature.

Deputies serve as your "eyes and ears" in the field. They can report on employee concerns, relay their questions to you, and enforce your rules and recommendations in a firm but polite manner. They're loyal, reliable individuals who share your commitment to pounce on problems early.

problems because they watch for the earliest signs of distress and come to the rescue. When they hear an employee say, "Oh, it's just as isolated incident," they know better than to accept such an assurance at face value. When they spot a minor blip in sales figures or notice a few workers not following directions, they find out why rather than walk away. They may adopt a wait-and-see attitude on occasion, but they usually prefer to root out answers so they can make faster, smarter decisions.

Speaking of attitude, the way in which you mentally approach setbacks sets the tone for what you're going to face next. Stand tall in the face of adversity. Resist the urge to complain, lose your temper, or resort to pointing fingers. Employees look to you for guidance. By anticipating problems and taking bold, definitive steps to prevent them, you empower everyone to follow your lead.

Manager's Checklist for Chapter 11

❏ Assemble a team of five to 10 "solution czars" who will help you prevent problems.

❏ When something's amiss, acknowledge it and determine ways to correct it. Don't assume a problem will go away on its own.

❏ Devise a ranking system to prioritize your work. Confront problems in sequence, starting with the most pressing, to prevent them from gaining momentum.

❏ Share your feelings and concerns honestly with employees—and listen to theirs. Speak in positive language without undue fretting. Ignoring or suppressing problems almost guarantees they'll get worse.

❏ When you level with employees about what's wrong, consider the situation from their perspective before you say a word. That way, you don't shoot from the hip.

❏ Apply critical reasoning skills so that you separate fact from assumption and listen more closely.

Index

A

Advice
  open mind and, 38
  pitfalls and, 37-38
  seeking, 36-37
  tool for asking, 37
Ambiguity, reducing, 48-50
Analyze, then judge, 91-93
"A players", 96
Assumptions and misunderstanding
  have shared understanding of words used, 45-46
  other people listen to you, 46
  other people want to understand you, 46-47
Attitude
  centered, 6
  in dealing with problems, 5-7
  gloomy, 5
  optimistic, 5
  problem-solvers vs. problem-creators, 105-106
  wait and see, 2-3
Autry, James A. (*Life and Work*), 1
Axelrod, Beth (*The War for Talent*), 96

B

Battles
  framing conflict as, 75-76
  war metaphors, eliminating, 76
Benefits, after layoff, 131
Biases, understanding personal, 146
Blame/fault for problems, 87-88
"BMW" (bitches, moans, whines), 89-91
Body language, and misunderstanding, 52
Bush, George W., 39

C

Calendar, use of in analyzing problem, 6
Causes of problems
  categories, 86-89
  labeling, 86
Change
  as cause of stress, 111
  celebrating small wins during, 115-117
  communication, importance in, 112-115
  dread of, 108
  earning employee buy-in, 113, 119-120
  employee resistance, 109-110, 120
  "I" predictions and, 115
  as indication of something being wrong, 110-111
  making worst of, 117

1-3-6 communication tool,
  113
  preparing employees for, 110
  and projections gone awry,
    114-115
  from resistance to acceptance,
    118-120
  survivors, 109
  three myths of, 109-111
Celebrating wins, methods, 116-
  117
Checking in, importance of, 48
Clarity vs. understanding, 47
Cloke, Kenneth (*Resolving
  Conflicts at Work*), 102
Communication
  changes in, as clue of problem,
    9
  checkpoints to ensure under-
    standing, 51
  keeping log of changes in, 10
  and problem prevention, 136-
    137
  sloppy skills in, and problems,
    144-145
  talking out concerns, 141
  words that motivate, 142
  writing tips, 128
  written, importance of, 128-
    129
Complaining, negative effects of,
  89
Conflict
  as battles, 75-76
  becoming indignant, 77
  between employees, three
    questions, 17
  grudges and, 17
  and "right warriors," 17-18
  seven biggest, 68-80
*Control Your Destiny or Someone
  Else Will* (Tichy), 89

Conversation
  body language and, 53
  letting others have the last
    word, 52
  listen to make sense, 43
  techniques to ensure under-
    standing, 47-48
  using questions to advance, 42
Counsel, wise, checklist for, 37
"C players", problem of, 96
Critical thinking, in evaluating
  employees, 145
Criticism, dealing with, 78

D
Daly, Chuck, 92-93
Daydreaming, and listening, 44
Defensive pessimism
  defined, 62
  three-step process of, 62-63
deGaulle's (Charles) rules, 63
  strategy for using, 64-65
Denial, 22-24, 83
"Deputies," and problem prevention, 147
Difficult vs. different, 100-101
Discipline
  appropriate, 66-67
  how to, 67
  on humanizing, 66
Duck, Jeanie Daniel, on change,
  109

E
eConnections Inc., 5
80-10 formula, for pondering
  problems, 97
Either/or bind, 88-89
Emotions
  advantages of controlling, 56-
    57
  anger management, 57
  assessing source of discord, 59

describing feelings, 57
example of poor control, 58
Hess, Jon, on, 68-69
Kramer, Michael, on, 68-69
management of, 69
negative effects, reducing, 56
rational vs. irrational, 58
reasons for feelings, 58-59
second opinion on, 59
three A's of, 57
Employee contribution and profit
link, 130
rules to facilitate, 130
Enron, and ignoring problems, 24
Ethics
abuse of power and, 11-12
gifts and, 13
jumbled priorities and, 11
misguided incentives and, 11
outside activities and, 13
and protecting proprietary
information, 12-13
quiz, 12
safeguarding company assets
and, 13
as source of problems, 11-13

F
Feedback that gets results, 133-
134
Foch, Ferdinand, quoted, 76

G
Gergen, Kenneth, quoted, 94
Goldsmith, Joan (*Resolving
Conflicts at Work*), 102
Gossip and problems, 99
Grievance, five-step process for
expressing, 60-61
"Groda" (Get rid of dangerous
ambiguities), 48-50
Grudge
dealing with effectively, 60-61

getting past, 59-61
Gut instinct, misguided faith in,
97-98

H
Handfield-Jones, Helen (*The War
for Talent*), 96
*Harvard Management
Communication Letter*, 94
Harvard Management Update, 26
Hess, Jon, on emotions, 68-69
*How to Make the Most of Your
Workday* (Pickering), 140

I
Impending trouble, clues of, 2
Impulsiveness
defined, 144
and poor decision making, 145
Indignation
limiting, 77-78
as problem source, 77
Information, asking for, 50
Instructions, care in giving, 99

J
Judge, when to, 92

K
Kramer, Michael, on emotions,
68-69
Kuhn, Thomas (*The Structure of
Scientific Revolutions*), 109

L
Learned helplessness, described,
102
Life and Work (Autry), 1
Listening
daydreaming as barrier to, 43
to learn, steps for, 42-43
for mutual understanding, 99
paraphrasing and, 44
poor, as cause of miscom-
muncation, 42

to prevent misunderstanding, 42
selective, 25

M
Manzoni, Jean-Francois, quoted, 26
Martinez, Arthur (CEO, Sears), 91, 93
Michaels, Ed (*The War for Talent*), 96
Misunderstandings
assumptions contributing to, 45-47
checking in with speaker, 44
multitasking and, 50
preventing, 41-54
wait before responding, 43
Morale, post-layoff, 129-131
Motivation
empowering and, 130
and lack of commitment, 123-124
after layoff, 129-131
and money, 123
and rewards, 123
and three-question rule, 125
writing tips for, 128
Murphy's Law, 70

N
Negative thinking
checklist for, 63
defensive pessimism, 62-63
value of, 61-63
Norem, Julie K. (*The Positive Power of Negative Thinking*), 61

P
Paradigm shift, defined, 109
Paraphrasing
phrases for, 45
to reduce misunderstanding, 44

Parker, James (CEO, Southwest Airlines), 124
Pause, three-second, 98
Peale, Norman Vincent (*The Power of Positive Thinking*), 61
Performance reviews, PAID method, 133-134
Peters, Tom, 26
Pickering, Peg (*How to Make the Most of Your Workday*), 140
Pike, Bob, on problem sharing, 39
Pilots, jet, 1
Poor performers, failure to manage, 95-96
The Positive Power of Negative Thinking (Norem), 61
Powell, Colin, quoted, 15
The Power of Positive Thinking (Peale), 61
Praise, refusal to, 96
Praise/criticism ratio, 133
Projection, defined, 8
Probability
and problem variables, 6-7
and realistic expectations about problems, 6-7
Problem management, three D's, 3-5
Problem prevention
and contingency planning, 142-144
"deputies" and, 147
questions to ask, 137
"solution czars" and, 138-139
talking out concerns and, 141
template for, 147
thinking ahead and, 146
"trackers" and, 147
Problems
accepting, as first step, 83
acknowledging scope, 24
acting vs. stewing, 34-36

advice, asking for, 36-37
anger and, 23
approval dependence, as
    source of, 146
assessment, levels of, 25
"BMW" (bitching, moaning,
    whining) response, 89-91
collecting solutions from
    employees, 27, 38
as communication breakdown,
    41
deGaulle's (Charles) rules for
    responding, 64-65
denial and, 22-24, 83
describing effectively, 71
dwelling on the past and, 35
fake and real, 7-8
fear and creation of, 104-105
first reactions, 82
gossip, as source of, 99
half-hearted attempts to solve,
    21-22
helping employees deal with,
    124
ignoring, 18
keeping record of, tool for, 23
labeling cause, 86-89
learning from, five steps, 20
making minor into major, 8
managers as responsible for,
    144
mobilizing action to solve, 26-
    27
as opportunity, 61
out of control, dealing with,
    70-72
preventing, strategy for, 136-
    148
profile, six stages of, 15-27
promises, broken, as source
    of, 74-75
question to ask, 26

rationalization and, 19
react vs. respond, 55-56
reacting as scientist, 81-93
resurfacing, 22
rule changes as indication of,
    10-11
scenarios, exercise, 3
as self-fulfilling prophecy, 103
summary, writing, 84-86
system for solving, 29-34
traps for creating, 95-98
visualization and, 20
Problem-solvers vs. problem-
    creators
difference defined, 95, 101
and expressing good news,
    105-106
fear and, 104-105
future predictions and, 103
problem-creation traps, 95-98
thinking before talking, 98
Procrastination, "three to five"
    rule, 34
Promises
broken, dealing with, 74-75
toning down, 97

R
Reagan, Ronald, 72
Resolving Conflicts at Work
    (Cloke and Goldsmith), 102
Rodin, Robert (CEO,
    eConnections Inc.), 5
Rumors, stopping, 131

S
Schwab, Charles (CEO,
    Bethlehem Steel), 139-140
Science and response to prob-
    lems, 82
Seligman, Martin, on learned
    helplessness, 102
Servant leadership, 119

Silo mentality, defined, 141
Simmons, Annette, on practical problem solving, 102
"Solution czars," methodology, 138-139
Solution to problems
anchoring bias and, 30
choosing best, 32-33
coworker help in implementing, 38
execution of, 33-34
four steps for, 29-34
grading ideas for, 31-32
group buy-in and, 38-39
identifying options, 29
and infusing energy into employees, 35
measurable criteria for, 31-32
and proactive managers, 140
wise counsel and, 36-37
Stress
and change, 111
tool for measuring, 112
The Structure of Scientific Revolutions (Kuhn), 109
Summarizing problems
example, 85
how to, 84-86

T
Three D's of problem mismanagement
battling, 3-5
dismissing, 5
distorting, 4
downplaying 4
Three-second pause, 98
Tichy, Noel (*Control Your Destiny or Someone Else Will*), 89
Time
mental clock, repositioning, 70
90-10 formula and, 97

as source of conflict, 69-70
"Trackers," and problem prevention, 147
Trouble
clues of occurrence, 8-11
communication changes, 9
pattern disruption, 9-10
rule changes, 10-11
rushing into, 50-51
Trust
breakdown, 72
building, steps for, 73-74
Truth, fudging, 96-97

U
Underdogs, using to advantage, 132
Upheaval at the top, surviving, 117-118

W
Want/can't have situation, 86-87
The War for Talent (Michaels, Handfield-Jones, and Axelrod), 96
Wilkens, Lenny, 92
Words, long-remembered, 100
Workers, lower-level, winning over, 125-127
Work habits, based on sound reasoning, 145
Worst case
planning for, 2-3
impending trouble, clues, 2
wait-and-see attitude, 2-3
Written communication
importance of, 128-129
reading between the lines, 128
tips for, 128
Wrong vs. right
as problem source, 78-79
resolving, 79

About the Author

Morey Stettner is a writer and communication-skills consultant in Portsmouth, NH. He's the author of another popular Briefcase Book, *Skills for New Managers* (McGraw-Hill, 2000), as well as *The Art of Winning Conversation* (Prentice Hall, 1995). A dynamic speaker and seminar leader, he has led hundreds of training programs across the United States on topics such as sales skills, public speaking, and effective listening. He graduated magna cum laude from Brown University. You can e-mail him at may12@concentric.net.